James K. Baxter: The Selected Poems

James K. Baxter
The Selected Poems

edited by John Weir

TE HERENGA WAKA
UNIVERSITY PRESS

Cold Hub Press

Te Herenga Waka University Press
Victoria University of Wellington
PO Box 600, Wellington
New Zealand
teherengawakapress.co.nz

Cold Hub Press
PO Box 156, Lyttelton
New Zealand
coldhubpress.co.nz

ISBN 978-1-77692-075-4

A catalogue record is available from
the National Library of New Zealand.

Printed in Singapore by Markono Print Media Pte Ltd.

Contents

Return to Dunedin 1966–1968

Introduction

James Keir Baxter was, by any standards, a remarkably prolific poet. This selection has been made from the more than three thousand poems which comprise his literary legacy.

Baxter was born in Dunedin on 29 June 1926 and spent most of his boyhood at Brighton, a small coastal settlement which was the hub of a farming community seventeen kilometres from the city. He began writing poetry when he was a seven-year-old pupil at the local primary school and may already have been aware of the fact that his parents (a renowned pacifist father and a highly academic mother) were very different from the other parents in the village and district.

In any case, while he was at primary school he perceived himself to be an outsider, later disclosing that

> a sense of grief has attached itself to my early life, like a tapeworm in the stomach of a polar bear . . . the sense of having been pounded all over with a club by invisible adversaries is generally with me, and has been with me as long as I can remember. . . . A sense of grief – even at times a sense of grievance – helped me to write poems. In a way the poems sprang out of a quarrel with the status quo.[1]

In 1937 the Baxters sailed to England where they visited the site of Sling Camp in Wiltshire where Archibald Baxter was interned and treated shamefully during World War One. At times the family travelled together in England, Scotland and Europe, but, for the greater part, James and his elder brother Terry boarded at a Quaker school at Sibford Ferris in the Cotswolds. Yet again, James experienced loneliness and alienation, but he also found, in his English teacher, an appreciative and encouraging reader for his poetry.

After the family returned to New Zealand in 1938 James felt even more out of place than previously – his literary interests and his family's pacifism set them apart from their neighbours. Both at Brighton and at King's High School in South Dunedin (which he began attending early in 1940) during a particularly painful adolescence his sense of being at odds with himself and the world became even more pronounced. Isolated, he channelled his thoughts and conversation into poems and began entering them into manuscript books. Many years later he wrote about this:

> I think the sense of a gap between myself and other people was increased considerably by the fact that I was born in New Zealand, and grew up there till I was nine, and then attended an English boarding-school for a couple of years, and came back to New Zealand at thirteen, in the first flush of puberty, quite out of touch with my childhood companions and uncertain whether I was an Englishman or a New Zealander. This experience too, though very painful, was beneficial; for I fell into the habit of poem-writing with a vengeance and counted it a poor week when I had not written four or five pieces of verse.[2]

In fact, he wrote hundreds of poems during those early years.

In December 1941 Terry was detained by the authorities for following in his father's footsteps and refusing to fight in a war. In the next year he became a friend of Noel Ginn, a fellow-detainee who wrote poetry, and when he told Ginn that his younger brother was also a poet the two began a correspondence. James's introductory letter unlocked a four year long flood of poems and commentary, for Ginn was now virtually the only audience he had for his poetry and his ideas about literature and composition. By this time he had written more than six hundred poems – most from the boundless recesses of his imagination, few from experience. He was a voracious reader of poetry (he later described himself as 'the book-bred one') and he was not at all reticent when it came to offering Ginn his critical opinion.

At Otago University, where he enrolled in March 1944 in English, Latin, French and Philosophy, he showed every sign of becoming a poet of great distinction, but he also proved to be a poor student, with the result that he left after just one year. In his 'Essay on the Higher Learning' he described his progress as an undergraduate:

> Good things came to me from Otago. My incipient alcoholism took wings like a bush fire, leaping fence and river, in the Bowling Green, the Royal Albert, the Captain Cook, the Grand, the City, the Oban, the Shamrock (on Sundays) and the Robert Burns (my best friend had a flat above it). The

Furies, those Muses of black-humour poetry, roosted on my doorstep like great scraggy chickens, and never left it again. It is, after all, their proper home. A female medical student taught me another kind of knowledge in her Castle Street lodgings . . .

God also, whom I had not met till then, revealed Himself to me one day when I had reached the middle of a disused railway tunnel, in the grip of a brutal hangover. But was any of this a necessary part of the Higher Learning? It is hard to say. Aphrodite, Bacchus, and the Holy Spirit were my tutors, but the goddess of good manners and examination passes withheld her smile from me.[3]

When he left university he did so in the knowledge that his first poetry collection was about to be ushered into print. *Beyond the Palisade* (1944) was a remarkable first book, but it also reveals the influence of his reading, for echoes abound of French Symbolists, English pre-Romantics, Romantics and some moderns. Even so, it was plain to see that a major new talent had emerged in New Zealand.

Between 1945 and 1948 he continued to live in and around Dunedin, doing manual work, having affairs, drinking heavily, hanging around the university and writing poetry, but the poems he wrote did not reflect his Bohemian lifestyle, for their literary forms were traditional, while their assured tone conveyed a sense of gravity and almost religious decorum. In 1948 when poems of this kind appeared in his second book, *Blow, Wind of Fruitfulness*, readers could be forgiven for thinking that they were composed by someone whose life and convictions were settled and serene, but nothing could have been further from the truth.

At the end of that year, 'after much apparently useless experience in various factories, farms, dens, bedrooms, pubs and hovels' and energised by a compulsion to escape from his mother's oversight, to consult a psychologist and otherwise to work matters out for himself, he moved from Dunedin to Christchurch, where he 'lived inside the spiritual bomb-shelters erected by Rimbaud, Dylan Thomas and Hart Crane' while 'The irrigating river of alcohol flowed continually' through his veins. He found work at times, came to know the poets Allen Curnow and Denis Glover, and was received into the Church of England. It was, he remarked, 'unquestionably a seeding-time, when I became a man of sorts and ploughed under everything I had ever known, as a farmer ploughs in autumn before the hard frosts arrive'.[4]

In December 1948 he married Jacqueline Sturm and moved to Wellington where he worked in an abattoir and as a postman before becoming a primary school teacher. During the training period and in the course of the two years teaching which followed it, he persevered with part-time study at Victoria University, and in May 1956, despite his professed distaste for academia, he graduated with a Bachelor of Arts. In the same month he gained employment as a writer and editor for the Publications Branch of the Department of Education.

During the late 1940s and 1950s his poetic output had lessened as he concentrated on achieving technical excellence, with the result that some of the gravely rhetorical poems which he wrote indicated that an immensely talented young poet was practising his craft in New Zealand. (The most significant poems in his 1953 publication *The Fallen House*, like those in *Blow, Wind of Fruitfulness*, consider the complexity and pain of existence, while sounding a note of lamentation for the passing of time and the loss of innocence and tranquillity.)

Notwithstanding their fluency and technical excellence, his poems were often still too derivative, for he had found it difficult to transcend the influences of W. B. Yeats, Thomas Hardy, George Barker, and Dylan Thomas. He had not yet found his own true voice.

In 1954 he made a life-changing decision and joined Alcoholics Anonymous, committing himself wholeheartedly to its principles and programmes and working generously in support of other alcoholics. A little later his awareness of his need for spiritual regeneration and moral redemption compelled him to make another long-considered change, as a result of which, late in 1957, he began a course of instruction in the Roman Catholic faith. In the following January he was received into the Church.

In 1958 he was awarded a UNESCO Fellowship which made it possible for him to travel to Japan to attend a conference on teaching resources. When it ended he went to India, where he was greatly moved by the plight of the urban poor. That visit made him increasingly critical of the dehumanising aspects of contemporary Western culture.

In the same year his stature as a poet was recognised internationally when Oxford University Press published a selection of his poetry under the title *In Fires of No Return*. In retrospect, these poems reveal that during the five-year period between 1953 and 1958 he had formulated or confirmed several of the perspectives which would shape the manner in which he lived for the remainder of his life.

Although he did not write consistently well during the 1950s – partly because of difficulties he experienced in reforming his life after coming off the grog in third-stage alcoholism, and partly because he had not yet found his own poetic voice – during the decade of the 1960s he wrote convincing verse narratives of the many tensions and little deaths which he experienced. This new-found strength is apparent in *Pig Island Letters* (1966) where, in eloquent, sinewy verse leavened by ambiguity, he dwelt upon the wounds which afflict people's lives. In this respect, the writers who affected him most positively were Louis MacNeice and Lawrence Durrell.

In 1966 when he was awarded the Robert Burns Fellowship at the University of Otago he returned to the province in which he grew up, where the bare coast reminded him of his spiritual origins:

Sitting down to write in a room in Wellington, again and again my mind would make an imaginary journey over the neck of the Big Rock, across the mouth of the Brighton River, and wander round the domain, or up to the boathouse, or along the sandhills, or out to the fishing rocks where the swells come straight in without interruption all the way from Peru. And my company would be the living and the dead — the living whom I had known while I was growing up, or the dead whom I had very often not known yet relied on for a sense of continuity and spiritual support.[5]

During these three years in Dunedin, haunted by visions of an earlier self and provoked by the spirit of the place where his forebears now gathered in memory, he explored his reactions in resonant, often elegiac verse.

However, by this time he was also beginning to feel that he should jettison his poetry-making habit and respond instead to the obvious needs in the lives of people he knew and within society at large. He had long exercised a personal ministry of practical help and support for his fellow-alcoholics, but at this time he felt compelled to minister to a larger group of people, whose needs, he believed, were not being met in middle-class

New Zealand. Within a short time he made a defining choice to enter and inhabit that world of destitution and oppressive need.

At the end of 1968 an event occurred which heralded the last phase of his life. In a dream he heard the call 'Go to Jerusalem!' – a small Māori settlement on the Whanganui River – and faithful to that summons he left Dunedin with only a change of clothes and part of a bible in Māori.

Before taking up residence in Jerusalem in 1969 he engaged in social work in Auckland among drug-addicts, alcoholics, the homeless and the unemployed. He claimed to have come to a realisation that he was 'steadily dying in the comfort of [his] home, smoking cigars and watching television' while there existed 'a really gross and obvious need for some of the people who [were] getting pulled to pieces in the towns to have a sanctuary'.[6] Recognising that 'the smashed myths have somehow to be replaced or reconstructed' he then established at Jerusalem a therapeutic community which offered a home to the marginalised and the emotionally wounded. One result of this was that he became a self-confessed 'Christian guru, a barefooted and bearded eccentric, a bad smell in the noses of many good citizens'.

He had renounced the ownership of property and taken a vow of poverty. Subsequently, during his frequent and memorable forays from Jerusalem to the cities and towns of New Zealand, he often spoke in favour of the reconstruction of the social order, his most insistent theme being that 'One of the great crimes of society is to be poor'.

He was also a willing partner in a number of sexual liaisons. While most of these were consensual, there were at least two which can be classified as rape. While the revelation of this fact has quite properly caused severe damage to his reputation as a man, it should also be said that, despite his preoccupation with sex and despite the serious offences he committed, he also gave direction and compassionate assistance to hundreds of people, young and old.

His life at Jerusalem is recorded in *Jerusalem Sonnets* (1970), *Jerusalem Daybook* (1971) and *Autumn Testament* (1972). In these late poems it is apparent that his lifelong search for integrity and his painful awareness of his flaws had finally caused him to abandon whatever traces of rhetoric still persisted in his verse. He found subject matter for his poetry in imme-diate, everyday events and blurred the border between poetry and prose.

His disarmingly simple words and phrases not only embody the simplicity and freedom he sought and, to some degree, found in his own life, they also brought a quality of lightness into the structure of his poems. Plain, forthright, angry, compassionate, wry, self-mocking, the Jerusalem poems give authentic expression to the experiences and the convictions of a passionate, complex and haunted man.

The announcement of his death in Auckland on Sunday, 22 October 1972, at the age of forty-six, generated a widespread grief because he had touched many lives and inspired many people. He was buried at Jerusalem, having bequeathed to New Zealanders a blueprint for social reconstruction based on Christian and Māori cultural values and a body of poetry and prose which was remarkable for its range and for the sense of a life lived here, in Aotearoa New Zealand.

In 1964 he described Louis MacNeice's last book as 'a summing-up, a paying of bills left long unpaid, personal rather than political.' He also remarked that 'There is deep melancholy at things out of joint, a sense of loss, but no abatement of courage. It is, from the most human of poets, an entirely human testament.'[7] His words capture the essence of his own best poems. In the last ten years of his life he acquired his own voice, and from his various quarrels with God, self, society and death emerged a body of work which reveals him to be not merely the most accessible and complete poet to have lived in New Zealand, but also one of the great English-language poets of the twentieth century.

*

Some selections of poems include pieces chiefly intended to illustrate a particular aspect of a poet's work (theme, style, literary affinities), but the basis of this selection is different, as it includes only what I consider to be the best or most recognisable poems Baxter wrote. In this sense I intended it to be read in the light of the tradition of a 'Best Poems'.

I am especially indebted to four people whose kindness and expertise have made the publication of this book possible. They are: John Baxter, who has given permissions and invaluable support; Roger Hickin, Editor at Cold Hub Press, for his enormous contribution to its production; Fergus Barrowman, Publisher at Te Herenga Waka University Press, who initiated and always believed in the Baxter project; and Cathy Harrison, whose generous and unfailing support enabled me to make what might well be my final foray into the field of Baxter studies which has occupied me, off and on, for more than fifty years.

References

1. 'Notes on the Education of a New Zealand Poet', *The Man on the Horse*, University of Otago Press, Dunedin, 1967, 217; *Complete Prose, Volume 2*, 217.
2. Ibid., 219.
3. 'Essay on the Higher Learning', *The Spike*, Victoria University of Wellington, 1961, 61–64; *Complete Prose, Volume 1*, 483–84.
4. Ibid., 484.
5. 'On Returning to Dunedin', *Otago Daily Times*, 22 September 1966, 4; *Complete Prose, Volume 2*, 97.
6. 'Poet. Philosopher and Commune Patriarch', *Auckland Star*, 23 October 1972.
7. NZ *Listener* 1272, 4 February 1964, 18; *Complete Prose, Volume 1*, 662–63.

James K. Baxter: The Selected Poems

Inscription

Within that land there is a range,
And on that range there is a cone,
And on that cone there is a rock,
And in that rock there is a cave,
And in that cave there is a stone,
And on that stone I carved a name,

And the cut letters will remain
At length when there are no more men
But only a little dust fallen
On gully, rock and cone.

High Country Weather

Alone we are born
   And die alone;
Yet see the red-gold cirrus
   Over snow-mountain shine.

Upon the upland road
   Ride easy, stranger:
Surrender to the sky
   Your heart of anger.

Lie deep, my love

Lie deep, my love, and listen now
To loud surf groaning in the strait –
The frail tree trembles under weight
Of brooding darkness on the bough:
And deeper shall your body lie
Where neither moon nor sun is known;
Heart sheds her living sympathy
Yielding dominion to the bone.

Yet in my touch forget all fears:
The timeless tumult in the vein
Makes minute hour, though late in pain
The clock was numbered with your tears.
Rain shakes the roofs – I cannot sleep
But turn the leaves of infancy
Remembered streams I could not keep –
Until you turn and compass me.

Blow, wind of fruitfulness

Blow, wind of fruitfulness
  Blow from the buried sun:
Blow from the buried kingdom
  Where heart and mind are one.

Blow, wind of fruitfulness,
  The murmuring leaves remember;
For deep in doorless rock
  Awaits their green September.

Blow from the wells of night:
  The blind flower breathes thy coming
Birds that are silent now
  And buds of barren springing.

Blow from beyond our day.
  The hill-born streams complain;
Hear from their stony courses
  The great sea rise again.

Blow on the mouth of morning
  Renew the single eye:
And from remembered darkness
  Our immortality.

Returned Soldier

The boy who volunteered at seventeen
At twenty-three is heavy on the booze.
Strafed in the desert and bombed out in Crete –
With sore dark eyes and hardened by the heat

Entitled now to call himself a man
And in the doll's-house walk with death at ease:
The Cairo women, cobbers under sand
A death too great for dolls to understand.

Back to a city bed or station hut
At maelstrom centre falling through the night
To dreams where deeper than El Alamein
A buried childhood stirs with leaves and flowers
Remembered girls, the blurred and bitter waters.
Wakes to the midnight rafters and the rain.

The Bay

On the road to the bay was a lake of rushes
Where we bathed at times and changed in the bamboos.
Now it is rather to stand and say:
How many roads we take that lead to Nowhere,
The alley overgrown, no meaning now but loss:
Not that veritable garden where everything comes easy.

And by the bay itself were cliffs with carved names
And a hut on the shore beside the Maori ovens.
We raced boats from the banks of the pumice creek
Or swam in those autumnal shallows
Growing cold in amber water, riding the logs
Upstream, and waiting for the taniwha.

So now I remember the bay and the little spiders
On driftwood, so poisonous and quick.
The carved cliffs and the great outcrying surf
With currents round the rocks and the birds rising.

A thousand times an hour is torn across
And burned for the sake of going on living.
But I remember the bay that never was
And stand like stone and cannot turn away.

Sea Noon

The grey smoke of rain drifts over headlands
And clear drops fall on the paper as I write.
Only the light thunder and murmur
Of ebbing and flowing furrows is endlessly repeated
And the rapid gulls flash over without sound.

Where is a house with windows open to the afternoon?
With light beer on tables and tobacco smoke
Floating; with a fire in the grate;
With music and the mind-filling pleasure of easy company.
Lying back in a chair to laugh or standing and smiling
One would accept all fates, and even the gold
Melancholy leaves of late autumn
Would seem as natural as a child's toy.

But labour and hunger strides the year
In seasonal repetition, more harsh than tidal waters.
The very rocks are cold: and they were lava once.

So stand the dull green trees bearing the weather
On solitary boughs; so the grey smoke of rain
Drifts on a painted verge of sea and air.
The fisherman casts his net to hold the tide.
Chilly the light wind blowing. And dark the face of noonday
As at the inconsolable parting of friends.

Naseby

Unchanging mountain scars
    Carry their mane of snow.
So for a thousand years
    The yellow broom will blow.

When the great wave is spent
    And earthquake broods no longer,
And iron armament
    Has fed an ocean hunger –

When, darkness on their breast
    Lover by lover lie,
And soldier calm at rest
    Knows not his enemy –

Then the dark peaks will hold
    Their peace beyond our knowing,
While over sunken gold
    The yellow broom is blowing.

Elegy for my Father's Father

He knew in the hour he died
That his heart had never spoken
In eighty years of days.
O for the tall tower broken
Memorial is denied:
And the unchanging cairn
That pipes could set ablaze
An aaronsrod and blossom.

They stood by the graveside
From his bitter veins born
And mourned him in their fashion.
A chain of sods in a day
He could slice and build
High as the head of a man
And a flowering cherry tree
On his walking shoulder held
Under the lion sun.
When he was old and blind
He sat in a curved chair
All day by the kitchen fire.
Many hours he had seen
The stars in their drunken dancing
Through the burning-glass of his mind
And sober knew the green
Boughs of heaven folding
The winter world in their hand.
The pride of his heart was dumb.
He knew in the hour he died
That his heart had never spoken
In song or bridal bed.
And the naked thought fell back
To a house by the waterside
And the leaves the wind had shaken
Then for a child's sake:
To the waves all night awake
With the dark mouths of the dead.
The tongues of water spoke
And his heart was unafraid.

Let Time be still

Let Time be still
Who takes all things,
Face, feature, memory
Under his blinding wings.

That I hold again the green
Larch of your body
Whose leaves will gather
The springs of the sky.

And fallen from his cloud
The falcon find
The thigh-encompassed wound
Breasts silken under hand.

Though in a dark room
We knew the day breaking
And the rain-bearing wind
Cold matins making.

Sure it seemed
That hidden away
From the sorrowful wind
In deep bracken I lay.

Your mouth was the sun
And green earth under
The rose of your body flowering
Asking and tender
In the timelost season
Of perpetual summer.

Tunnel Beach

The waist-high sea was rolling
Thunder along her seven iron beaches
As we climbed down to rocks and the curved sand,
Drowned Lyonesse lay lost and tolling
Waiting the cry of the sun's phoenix
From the sea-carved cliffs that held us in their hand.

Forgotten there the green
Paddocks we walked an hour before,
The mare and the foal and the witch-tormented wood
And the flaked salt boughs, for the boughs of flame were seen
Of the first garden and the root
Of graves in your salt mouth and the forehead branded fire.

Through the rock tunnel whined
The wind, Time's hound in leash,
And stirred the sand and murmured in your hair.
The honey of your moving thighs
Drew down the cirrus sky, your doves about the beach
Shut out sea thunder with their wings and stilled the lonely air.

But O rising I heard the loud
Voice of the sea's women riding
All storm to come. No virgin mother bore
My heart wave eaten. From the womb of cloud
Falls now no dove, but combers grinding
Break sullen on the last inviolate shore.

Haast Pass

In the dense bush all leaves and bark exude
The odour of mortality; for plants
Accept their death like stones
Rooted for ever in time's torrent bed.

Return from here. We have nothing to learn
From the dank falling of fern spores
Or the pure glacier blaze that melts
Down mountains, flowing to the Tasman.

This earth was never ours. Remember
Rather the tired faces in the pub
The children who have never grown. Return
To the near death, the loves like garden flowers.

Letter to Noel Ginn II

Two years of silence – I take pen again
To write a rhyming letter. You'll forgive
The interim, and knowing how we live
From hand to mouth, a certain thread of pain
And bitterness that blurs the narrative.
My last was in a more romantic vein.

Our dreams take refuge from the men we are
And hide as flies do from the winter chill.
The lost traveller's dream under the hill
Remains with me when propping up a bar
Or in strange beds I do the body ill
To gratify a merciless guiding star.

'Th' expense of spirit . . .' Yet the spirit grows
By grieving for the sensual heart in chains.
Birth-pangs that we mistake for burial-pains
Give promise of the everlasting rose
Where bitter Loss consolidates its gains.
This is the answer that no question knows.

I have the letters that you wrote from camp
(Defaulters' camp, in case this should be read
By other men) where living men grew dead
In grey monotony. I was a lamp,
A kind of beacon to you then, you said –
Since then the wick has grown a trifle damp.

No man can play Aladdin all his life.
The oil is blood, although the flame be clear,
And world-annihilating djinns appear
Unasked-for at the falling of a leaf.
Or else the heart becomes a cinder – Fear
Is Art's companion, and the hermit Grief.

So poets learn to live like other men
For money, lovers, or the friends with whom
Music can animate a sunless room
And rouse the rumour of a different Sun
That shines the same though endless night draw on
And wakes the dead heart from its numbered tomb.

Perhaps I overstate the case – but I
Live by extremes. The madman and the saint
Have both (I fear) the same extremist taint,
And both are mad to Madame Butterfly.
Being no Francis, I can scarcely paint
A halo – 'poet's licence' is my cry.

[12]

It was my dearly held delusion once
That labouring men were better than their betters
And needed only to throw off their fetters
For Eden to return to Adam's sons.
Since then I've worked with them; and they're go-getters
Just like the Rev. Fraser – bless his bones.

An 8 hour day is not conducive to
The exercise of one's imagination.
So I have found alas that my true station
Is still among the academic crew
Whom I despised for undue cerebration
That leads to withering of the heart and thew.

No doubt I'll find a niche where I can grumble
About the clique that pay me for my pen,
And drink with other intellectual men,
And gain some slight prestige, however humble,
With a little bitter poem now and then
Until the first apocalyptic rumble:

And that will be the Bomb. I often think
Of the climb we made like beetles up a drain
From neanderthal, to be washed down again
In a flood of dirty water from the sink.
Lions and horses also sport a brain
But do not pine for a celestial stink.

From this high window I can see the swells
Roll in with their incessant cannonade
Upon that shore where once, a lonely child, I made
My own mythology of weeds and shells
And dreamed I heard from the green water shade
The pealing of sea drowned cathedral bells.

[13]

(While in bombed Germany the violent dream
Grew flesh and blood and tore a city down
Whose dazed survivors searching among stones
Can find the lichen hunger or the scream
Of mandrake pain, but never that first sun-
Flower of peace upon a lucid stream.)

And it is good to walk upon the sand
In winter when the dunes are hard and dry
With frost that binds an iron earth and sky.
Bone of my bone, the stubborn rocks withstand
The ebb and surge of grief. The ocean I
Once feared, I love more than the frozen land.

There is a kind of reconciliation
With buried selves and seasons, so to walk
And listen to the arrogant seabirds' talk
Who have no interest in our damnation,
And feel beyond those frosty hillocks the
Thunder of an obliterating sea.

To my Father

Today, looking at the flowering peach,
The island off the shore and waves that break
Quiet upon the rocks and level beach –
We must join forces, you and I, remake
The harbour silted and the city bombed
And all our hopes that lie now fire-entombed.

Your country childhood helped to make you strong,
Ploughing at twelve. I only know the man.
While I grew up more sheltered and too long

In love with my disease; though illness can
Impart by dint of pain a different kind
Of toughness to the predatory mind.

There is a feud between us. I have loved
You more than my own good, because you stand
For country pride and gentleness, engraved
In forehead lines, veins swollen on the hand;
Also, behind slow speech and quiet eye
The rock of passionate integrity.

You were a poet whom the time betrayed
To action. So, as Jewish Solomon
Prayed for wisdom, you had prayed
That you might have a poet for a son.
The prayer was answered; but an answer may
Confound by its exactness those who pray.

Finding no fault in you, I have been tempted
To stay your child. But that which broke
(Nature) the navel-cord, has not exempted
Even your light and sympathetic yoke.
It is in me your own true mettle shows;
Nor can we thus be friends till we are foes.

This you know well, but it will bear repeating -
Almost you are at times a second self;
Almost at times I feel your heart beating
In my own breast as if there were no gulf
To sever us. And you have seemed then rather
An out-of-time twin brother than a father.

So much is true; yet I have seen the time
When I would cut the past out, like a cancer,
Which now I must digest in awkward rhyme
Until I move 'in measure like a dancer'.
To know an age where all our loves have scope
It is too much for any man to hope.

You, tickling trout once in a water-race;
You, playing cards, not caring if you lost;
You, shooting hares high on the mountain face,
You, showing me the ferns that grow from frost,
You, quoting Burns and Byron while I listened,
You, breaking quartz until the mica glistened.

These I remember, with the wind that blows
Forever pure down from the tussock ranges;
And these remain, like the everlasting snows,
Changeless in me while my life changes;
These, and a thousand things that prove
You rooted like a tree in the land's love.

I shall compare you to the bended bow,
Myself the arrow launched upon the hollow
Resounding air. And I must go
In time, my friend, to where you cannot follow.
It is not love would hope to keep me young,
The arrow rusted and the bow unstrung.

We have one aim: to set men free
From fear and custom and the incessant war
Of self with self and city against city –
So they may know the peace that they were born for
And find the earth sufficient, who instead
For fruit give scorpions and stones for bread.

And I sit now beside the wishing-well
And drop my silver down. I will have sons
And you grandchildren yet to tell
Old tales despite the anger of the guns:
Leisure to stroll and see Him unafraid
Who walked with Adam once in the green shade.

Thrushes

Ten days I watched beside a thrushes' nest
In a thorn bush among the green flax
Till the young ones grew down on their backs
And feathers at length on the wings and unfledged breast.

First from the pale eggs they came naked out
Red-skinned and ugly, squawking to be fed –
All mouth and insatiable gut, you'd have said,
Five of them, each with the same hungry shout;

Though the parent birds could tell as they gulped and tore
Which was the one needed the worm most.
All day long they'd come, perch on a post,
Feed them and fly away again for more.

Till the time came, on the eleventh day,
When strangely they scrambled out like driven things;
Launched on the air with untried wings
They fell and rose again and fluttered away.

Four of them rode the warm ancestral air.
But one flew straight to the flax bush shade
And slid down heavy on a forked blade
And caught by the neck and hung and strangled there.

Elegy for an Unknown Soldier

There was a time when I would magnify
His ending; scatter words as if I wept
Tears not my own but man's. There was a time.
But not now so. He died of a common sickness.

Nor did any new star shine
Upon that day when he came crying out
Of fleshy darkness to a world of pain
And waxen eyelids let the daylight enter.

So felt and tasted, found earth good enough.
Later he played with stones and wondered
If there was land beyond the dark sea rim
And where the road led out of the farthest paddock.

Awkward at school, he could not master sums.
Could you expect him then to understand
The miracle and menace of his body
That grew as mushrooms grow from dusk to dawn?

He had the weight though for a football scrum
And thought it fine to listen to the cheering
And drink beer with the boys, telling them tall
Stories of girls that he had never known.

So when the War came he was glad and sorry,
But soon enlisted. Then his mother cried
A little, and his father boasted how
He'd let him go, though needed for the farm.

Likely in Egypt he would find out something
About himself, if flies and drunkenness
And deadly heat could tell him much – until
In his first battle a shell splinter caught him.

So crown him with memorial bronze among
The older dead, child of a mountainous island.
Wings of a tarnished victory shadow him
Who born of silence has burned back to silence.

The Cave

In a hollow of the fields, where one would least expect it,
Stark and suddenly this limestone buttress:
A tree whose roots are bound about the stones,
Broad-leaved, hides well that crevice at the base
That leads, one guesses, to the sunless kingdom
Where souls endure the ache of Proserpine.

Entering where no man it seemed
Had come before, I found a rivulet
Beyond the rock door running in the dark.
Where it sprang from in the heart of the hill
No one could tell: alone
It ran like Time there in the dank silence.

I spoke once and my voice resounded
Among the many pillars. Further in
Were bones of sheep that strayed and died
In nether darkness, brown and water-worn.
The smell of earth was like a secret language
That dead men speak and we have long forgotten.

The whole weight of the hill hung over me.
Gladly I would have stayed there and been hidden
From every beast that moves beneath the sun,
From age's enmity and love's contagion:
But turned and climbed back to the barrier,
Pressed through and came to dazzling daylight out.

Farmhand

You will see him light a cigarette
At the hall door careless, leaning his back
Against the wall, or telling some new joke
To a friend, or looking out into the secret night.

But always his eyes turn
To the dance floor and the girls drifting like flowers
Before the music that tears
Slowly in his mind an old wound open.

His red sunburnt face and hairy hands
Were not made for dancing or love-making
But rather the earth wave breaking
To the plough, and crops slow-growing as his mind.

He has no girl to run her fingers through
His sandy hair, and giggle at his side
When Sunday couples walk. Instead
He has his awkward hopes, his envious dreams to yarn to.

But ah in harvest watch him
Forking stooks, effortless and strong –
Or listening like a lover to the song
Clear, without fault, of a new tractor engine.

Virginia Lake

The lake lies blind and glinting in the sun.
Among the reeds the red-billed native birds
Step high like dancers. I have found
A tongue to praise them, who was dumb,
And from the deaf morass one word
Breaks with the voices of the numberless drowned.

This was the garden and the talking water
Where once a child walked and wondered
At the leaves' treasure house, the brown ducks riding
Over the water face, the four winds calling
His name aloud, and a green world under
Where fish like stars in a fallen heaven glided.

And for his love the eyeless statues moved
Down the shell paths. The bandstand set
On fire with music blazing at its centre
Was havened in his love.
The lichened elm was rafters overhead,
Old waves unlocked their gates for him to enter.

Who now lies dumb, the black tongue dry
And the eyes weighed with coins.
O out of this rock tomb
Of labyrinthine grief I start and cry
Toward his real day – the undestroyed
Fantastic Eden of a waking dream.

Rocket Show

As warm north rain breaks over suburb houses,
Streaming on window glass, its drifting hazes
Covering harbour ranges with a dense hood:
I recall how eighteen months ago I stood
Ankle-deep in sand on an Otago beach
Watching the fireworks flare over strident surf and bach,
In brain grey ash, in heart the sea-change flowing
Of one love dying and another growing.

For love grows like the crocus bulb in winter
Hiding from snow and from itself the tender
Green frond in embryo; but dies as rockets die
(White sparks of pain against a steel-dark sky)
With firebird wings trailing an arc of grief
Across a night inhuman as the grave,
Falling at length a dull and smouldering shell
To frozen dunes and the wash of the quenching swell.

There was little room left where the crowd had trampled
Grass and lupin bare, under the pines that trembled
In gusts from the sea. On a sandhillock I chose
A place to watch from. Then the rockets rose,
O marvellous, like self-destroying flowers
On slender stems, with seed-pods full of flares,
Raining down amber, scarlet, pennies from heaven
On the skyward straining heads and still sea-haven.
Had they brought death, we would have stood the same,
I think, in ecstasy at the world-end flame.

It is the rain streaming reminds me of
Those ardent showers, cathartic love and grief.
As I walked home through the cold streets by moonlight,

My steps ringing in the October night,
I thought of our strange lives, the grinding cycle
Of death and renewal come to full circle,
And of man's heart, that blind Rosetta stone,
Mad as the polar moon, decipherable by none.

Wild Bees

Often in summer, on a tarred bridge plank standing,
Or downstream between willows, a safe Ophelia drifting
In a rented boat – I had seen them come and go,
Those wild bees swift as tigers, their gauze wings a-glitter
In passionless industry, clustering black at the crevice
Of a rotten cabbage tree, where their hive was hidden low.

But never strolled too near. Till one half-cloudy evening
Of ripe January, my friends and I
Came, gloved and masked to the eyes like plundering desperadoes,
To smoke them out. Quiet beside the stagnant river
We trod wet grasses down, hearing the crickets chitter
And waiting for light to drain from the wounded sky.

Before we reached the hive their sentries saw us
And sprang invisible through the darkening air,
Stabbed, and died in stinging. The hive woke. Poisonous fuming
Of sulphur filled the hollow trunk, and crawling
Blue flame sputtered – yet still their suicidal
Live raiders dived and clung to our hands and hair.

O it was Carthage under the Roman torches,
Or loud with flames and falling timber, Troy!
A job well botched. Half of the honey melted
And half the rest young grubs. Through earth-black smouldering ashes

And maimed bees groaning, we drew out our plunder.
Little enough their gold, and slight our joy.

Fallen then the city of instinctive wisdom.
Tragedy is written distinct and small:
A hive burned on a cool night in summer.
But loss is a precious stone to me, a nectar
Distilled in time, preaching the truth of winter
To the fallen heart that does not cease to fall.

Venetian Blinds

When four years old he fell asleep between
Cold mountainous sheets in his grandfather's house,
The slatted blind let through a zebra light
Upon his pillow, moss grey, charnel green:
Nor the toy bear even could ward the mouse
Carving a secret stair, and the clubfoot faceless Night.

As he grew older, fought and cried and played
Indians under lupins by the eel-thronged river,
His daydream paths converged till one path led
Him out of childhood trembling and afraid
Toward a dream of Woman, touch and savour
Behind venetian blinds, of flesh and feather bed.

Till, shadow victory accomplished, he
Lay waking by a warm and casual side
To tie all threads in a knot of disillusion.
Meanwhile the average light, no mystery,
With morning fell down wounded through the wide
Green blinds on blinking eyes and the tangled sheets' confusion.

The Morgue

Each morning when I lit the coke furnace
Unwillingly I passed the locked door,
The room where Death lived. Shadowless infection
Looked from the blind panes, and an open secret
Stained even the red flowers in the rock garden
Flesh-fingered under the sanatorium wall.

And each day the patients coming and going
From light jobs, joking below the sombre pines,
Would pass without looking, their faces leaner
As if the wintry neighbourhood of Death
Would strip the shuddering flesh from bone. They shouted,
Threw clods at one another, and passed on.

But when at length, with stiff broom and bucket,
I opened the door wide – well, there was nothing
To fear. Only the bare close concrete wall,
A slab of stone, and a wheeled canvas stretcher.
For Death had shifted house to his true home
And mansion, ruinous, of the human heart.

Poem in the Matukituki Valley

Some few yards from the hut the standing beeches
Let fall their dead limbs, overgrown
With feathered moss and filigree of bracken.
The rotted wood splits clean and hard
Close-grained to the driven axe, with sound of water
Sibilant falling and high nested birds.

In winter blind with snow; but in full summer
The forest blanket sheds its cloudy pollen
And cloaks a range in undevouring fire.
Remote the land's heart. Though the wild scrub cattle
Acclimatised, may learn
Shreds of her purpose, or the taloned kea.

For those who come as I do, half-aware,
Wading the swollen
Matukituki waist-high in snow water,
And stumbling where the mountains throw their dice
Of boulders huge as houses, or the smoking
Cataract flings its arrows on our path –

For us the land is matrix and destroyer,
Resentful, darkly known
By sunset omens, low words heard in branches;
Or where the red deer lift their innocent heads
Snuffing the wind for danger,
And from our footfall's menace bound in terror.

Three emblems of the heart I carry folded
As charms against flood water, sliding shale:
Pale gentian, lily, and bush orchid.
The peaks too have names to suit their whiteness,
Stargazer and Moonraker,
A sailor's language and a mountaineer's.

And those who sleep in close bags fitfully
Besieged by wind in a snowline bivouac –
The carrion parrot with red underwing
Clangs on the roof by night, and daybreak brings
Raincloud on purple ranges, light reflected
Stainless from crumbling glacier, dazzling snow,

Do they not, clay in that unearthly furnace,
Endure the hermit's peace
And mindless ecstasy? Blue-lipped crevasse
And smooth rock chimney straddling – a communion
With what eludes our net – Leviathan
Stirring to ocean birth our inland waters?

Sky's purity; the altar cloth of snow
On deathly summits laid; or avalanche
That shakes the rough moraine with giant laughter;
Snowplume and whirlwind – what are these
But His flawed mirror who gave the mountain strength
And dwells in holy calm, undying freshness?

Therefore we turn, hiding our souls' dullness
From that too blinding glass: turn to the gentle
Dark of the human daydream, child and wife,
Patience of stone and soil, the lawful city
Where man may live, and no wild trespass
Of what's eternal shake his grave of time.

Thoughts of a Dying Calvinist

The night's foul with hail and sleet
As I lie cold in linen sheet
And sweat long but get no heat.
The fear of death confounds me.

I could lie ill though happ'd in clay,
For there in Crookieden they say
The fire eats flesh and soul away.
The fear of death confounds me.

A brief thirst that none can slake,
A brief word, a brief wake,
A brief road that all must take –
The fear of death confounds me.

About the bed my kindred cry;
The greedy gled has a moister eye.
Deil take their carrion hearts to fry!
The fear of death confounds me.

When Brother John the Elder died
They broke the housewall open wide
To get his glutton's corpse outside.
The fear of death confounds me.

The wedding guests their meal begin,
But the ghost that dies in deadly sin
Shall knock but never enter in.
The fear of death confounds me.

O thou my God, judge as thou art,
Conning each man's black-rotten heart,
Take thou this hour the sinner's part.
The fear of death confounds me.

And bid me, Andrew Crummock, rise
To see thy Face in paradise
Or sleep now with the beast that dies.
The fear of death confounds me.

The Fallen House

I took the clay track leading
From Black Bridge to Duffy's farm,
In no forefarer's footmark treading,
   Thus free, it would seem, from any harm
That could befall me – the kind of ill-luck charm
   That clings to a once-fair steading –

When South the sky thickened
And rain came pelter on the hill-scurf:
So in a grove (where the wind quickened
   Their young leaves like the mile-off surf)
Of gums I sheltered, whose roots had drained the turf
   Of life till a starved soil sickened.

But an older grief spoke plainly
From the green mound where thistle strewed
Her bearded gossamer. Ungainly
   The sprawled stones fire-blackened could
Recall man; though where the house stood
   Stands ragged thistle only.

It was not Woe that flaunted
Funereal plume and banner there,
Nor an Atridean doom that daunted
   The heart with a lidless gorgon stare;
But darker the cradling bluegums, sombre the air,
   By the wraith of dead joy haunted.

There once the murk was cloven
By hearthlight fondly flaring within:
Adamant seemed their hope and haven.

O Time, Time takes in a gin
The quick of being! Pale now and gossamer-thin
The web their lives had woven.

Boscastle

Yes; I know the steep street well
Falling aslant between mossed roofs;
The shop counter where they sell
Postcards; the cobbles worn in grooves
    By wagons – or I could tell

How the blowhole like a signal gun
Spouted upon the narrow bay.
As a child I went there; but no one
Told me a cast of uncommon clay
    Had walked under that sun.

The slateblue butterflies windblown
I saw, but no bent man
With large brow, standing alone
Wraithlike; though since, by Time's plan,
    His grief has seemed my own.

By Tintagel the clifftop path
Broke sudden at a sheer verge
Where sea-maned reefs groaned in wrath
And gulls cried dead Tristan's dirge –
    For the stumbler no aftermath.

A child's clear mind mirrored the show.
I slept, ate, read and talked
Without sense of a being's flow:

That on those stones Hardy had walked
Then I did not know.

In the Lecture Room

The lecturer's impartial prose
    Droned in the raftered room;
Through a mock-Gothic window rose
    The soft weir water's boom.

The blonde girl in the second bench
    Biting her pencil, sighed –
Thought 'If I lowered my frock an inch
    It would look well in that shade.'

The young man at the back, half-turning
    To see her profile, smiled;
Thought 'She has a scholar's learning
    And the innocence of a child.'

The clock in the college tower broke
    On sparrows' private lives:
The lecturer cleared his throat and spoke
    Of McDougall's instinctive drives;

Paused a moment in his talk,
    Massaged an itching wen,
Doodled a diagram in chalk
    And rubbed it off again.

Tarras Moon

When Tim and I stumbled
On the rough Tarras track
(We shared the station shack)
Blind drunk we fumbled
Like ferrets in a sack
Together tumbled,
That no way can fare.

I knew her not from a lantern
Or a lowe in the lift –
Grim in her graveshift
The bare poxy wanton,
Queen Death glowered from a rift
Of cloudwrack above the mountain,
Walking on wild air.

'Ripe archaic' her feature
From a Sicilian metope,
Two snakes for a knotted rope
About her middle: the creature
That eats our carrion hope:
Glass of malignant Nature,
Diana chastely fair.

'She's like my granny, but older
By a long chalk,' Tim said.
In a corpselight hither shed
Clear shone tussock and boulder:
Like men already dead
Under Mt Iron's shoulder
Moonstruck we staggered there.

Book of the Dead

Pollen-heavy the black bee
Above the flaring clematis drones;
Fennel and flax among the gravestones
Flourish, and rough cabbage-tree.
Stranger, of your charity
Pray for the souls
Of those hereunder
That they in light perpetual tarry.

'A bushman I; so rejoiced
When roots of laurel burst apart
Angel and cross, drove through my heart,
And the night grass murmured million-voiced.'
Stranger, of your charity
Pray for the soul
Of Harry Garnett
That he in light perpetual tarry.

'Dad thrashed me till I thrashed Dad.
At twenty-four an A.B.
A knife in the back at a mollhouse spree,
And my long home was the first I had.'
Stranger, of your charity
Pray for the soul
Of Nathan Carpenter
That he in light perpetual tarry.

'Loth was I to leave earth,
The house built newly, the gully farm
With my dear love ploughing; but beyond harm
The bones that proved too small for childbirth.'

Stranger, of your charity
Pray for the soul
Of Mary Hamilton
That she in light perpetual tarry.

'Din of no upland watercourse
Fills my dead ear; but the low sound
I heard as a lad from springs profound
That eddy at the Severn's source.'
    Stranger, of your charity
    Pray for the soul
    Of John Trevellyan
    That he in light perpetual tarry.

'A down-at-heel remittance man
From a good home; but better, this.
Friend, fare on. My tipple is
Not brandy but oblivion.'
    Stranger, of your charity
    Pray for the soul
    Of Hugh Beaumont
    That he in light perpetual tarry.

Not fifty yards from college and shop
Lie they, long ensepulchred.
Her wild wing earthward bending, a bird
Pecks for seed on the fennel top.
    Stranger, of your charity
    Pray for the souls
    Of these hereunder
    That they in light perpetual tarry.

The Bad Young Man

'Oh summer is a beggar's feast,'
  Cried the rumbustious bad young man,
'And Nobodaddy cares in the least
If we two make the two-backed beast –
So lie you down, lie you down!'
'I think my maiden aunt would frown,'
  She said under the yellow lupin.

'Gulls are tumbling on the wing,'
  Cried the rumbustious bad young man,
'And the little fishes have their fling:
So why should a scruple keep us waiting?
And O my dear, I love you so.'
'You'll tell a different tale tomorrow,'
  She said under the yellow lupin.

'O cover me with your tent of hair,'
  Groaned the rumbustious bad young man.
'Milk and honey, your breasts are bare,
My sucking dove, my silken mare –
Wherever you learnt it you have the knack.'
'Gentlier, or you'll break my back,'
  She moaned under the yellow lupin.

'Ah Love's joy was not made to last,'
  Sighed the rumbustious sad young man.
'The world's mill is grinding fast
And the sky, the sky is overcast –
But still, I thank you for your kindness.'
'I fear the sand has soiled my dress,'
  She said under the yellow lupin.

Portrait of a Poet

Despair in action, the Goya pictures, were
Pointed for him: in that context he understood
His first wife who wore death like a fur
And the second one who had him taped for good.

Or a Dostoevsky world where good and bad
Were interdependent, only the itch of grief
Absolute. It seemed somehow he had
Confused Christ with the Impenitent Thief.

Being separated from childhood by a crevasse
Deep as the grave, he would likely teach well;
Have a soft spot for the tough boy in the class,
And if he caught them canoodling never tell.

The big man with a glass of gin and fizz
Spilling in poems, in open wounds, the shame,
The importunate horror of knowing the world as it is,
Unpardonable, and loving it just the same.

The Homecoming

Odysseus has come home, to the gully farm
Where the macrocarpa windbreak shields a house
Heavy with time's reliques – the brown-filmed photographs
Of ghosts more real than he; the mankind-measuring arm
Of a pendulum clock; and true yet to her vows,
His mother, grief's Penelope. At the blind the sea wind laughs.

The siege more long and terrible than Troy's
Begins again. A love demanding all,
Hypochondriacal, sea-dark and contentless:

[36]

This was the sour ground that nurtured a boy's
Dream of freedom; this, in Circe's hall
Drugged him; his homecoming finds this, more relentless.

She does not say, 'You have changed'; nor could she imagine any
Otherwise to the quiet maelstrom spinning
In the circle of their days. Still she would wish to carry
Him folded within her, shut from the wild and many
Voices of life's combat, in the cage of beginning;
She counts it natural that he should never marry.

She will cook his meals; complain of the south weather
That wrings her joints. And he – rebels; and yields
To the old covenant – calms the bleating
Ewe in birth travail. The smell of saddle leather
His sacrament; or the sale day drink; yet hears beyond sparse fields
On reef and cave the sea's hexameter beating.

Never No More

Oh the summer's afloat on spindrift beaches
Brown as bread in a holiday heaven:
The same sweet lie the lupin teaches
As always dropping her gay pollen
On a girl's print frock leg shoulder bare
Never no more never no more.

The boys climb to their branch-high houses
Under a black bridge dive for pennies
The noon cloud like a bird's breast downy
Night come cool as a hawthorn berry
Kite tails tied on a telephone wire
Never no more never no more.

[37]

Cigarette stink from a hole in the rushes
Dark as a dunny the under-runner
The green flax plaited for whiplashes
Cockabully finned with the fire of summer
Jack loves Jill on the garage door
Never no more never no more.

The trodden path in the brambles led
Sweet and sure to a lifted frock
To the boathouse spree and the hayloft bed
A hamstrung heart and no way back:
Like a toetoe arrow shot in the air
Never no more never no more.

The Book of Hours

De Berry's *Book of Hours*: the four seasons
Frozen in equipoise on the coloured page.
Always above, the sungod's molten chariot
In a vault of indigo; below, the pageant
Of man and beast, community of labour,
Order of heart and hand – O pastoral dream
Of Renaissance spring! imagined, never actual
In this or any age.

Yet the tapestry moves in a wind freshly blowing
Across five centuries – see how the women yarn
Warming their bottoms at a blazing faggot
While the old man blows on his hands and curses the weather,
With pigeons hopping on snow, sheep dry in the fold;
How the court ladies innocently wanton
Stoop gathering wildflowers. Wheat and tares together
Are gathered, laid in the barn.

Nor has he exiled even the pagan terror,
The verb of suffering, ancestral fear.
Over the fields of March, vinetrimmers and stolid
Yoke of oxen, stands the fairytale castle
Crowned by a flying dragon; and in grey December
In a forest clearing hounds bay, the hunter's clarion
Tells of the stricken boar, the body mangled,
Death of the sylvan year.

No doubt it was never like that – the madonna-breasted
Ladies chattered their scandal; the peasant ploughed
His own heart under, poor, confined and slavish.
But the dream of peace remains, the past accusing
Our lives, infirm, unfertile. There is the dance
Of labour slow as harvest, the reconciliation
Of man to his dignity, the gift of the joyful Logos
That we have disavowed.

The Journey

Then, coming to the long ship, they stowed
Wineskins aboard, water from the sedgy creek,
With red apples, honey from the wild bees' hoard
By shepherds ransacked from a ravens' cleft
Where ivies tomb the twilight and the spider keeps
Vigil yearlong. All these, gifts of the goddess, were lashed
Under the rowers' benches – the bellowing ram also
And black ewe, on whose fleece the flung saltflake dries.

With handclasp, singing, and shed tears they take
Leave of Aeaea, the green isle summer-browed,
Isle of their drowsy feasting. With the sound of *never*,
The keel rasped on sand, rode, rocked on the greymaned wave.

Moaning and manybreasted, the whale's path lay
Westward, perilous, to Cimmeria the sunless
And Hades' silence. All eyes looked back.
Only Odysseus, in the ship's prow standing, did not turn or speak.

And like a stormbird through daylight and darkness
She fled, a serpent wake behind her coiling,
The sun a brazen shield, or clammy nightfogs drifting,
Till at the frontiers of the murmuring Dead
They beached, where poplar and lamenting willow
Let fall their vacant seed. There made
Sacrifice to Persephone, sprinkled the white barley.
The Dead gathered, like moths, with wrath and ululation.

Seraphion

I, Seraphion, hermit of Mount Athos,
Three hundred feet above the sea's mumble
Alone in a rock shelter, the sparrow's refuge
With a stone couch, one ikon and a lamp,
In the judgement of the eye of absolute Day
Await the hour of my death.

I, Seraphion, was once Demetrios
Singer of ballads, thief and actor.
Lord, let these swollen joints, back bruised by the scourge,
Eyes weak with tears and icy fasting,
Be acceptable sacrifice, sign of the penitent – Deliver,
O Lord, my soul alive!

This voice, whose psalms startle the gull, once
In wineshops won silver and applause; these knees, that bend
Hourly, in the pit of perfumed beds

Opened the thighs of harlots. In Alexandrian gardens,
In the brothels of Beirut, in the mire of Babylon
My invisible Enemy triumphed and trod me down.

Till in black night came One, the Shepherd, to wash me
Clean of the burning raddle. Let Him be praised:
With Him alone is power. I woke and fled
To the rock of Athos, shunning
All temporal beauty, solace of wall and vineyard
To praise Him in the desert of His Truth.

On Athos is no sight or sound of woman,
No female thing, no, not a pigeon cloistered
On monastery roofs. In this bare place
My hermitage, I see only at evening
The face of him who brings me water and lentils,
Kneels for my blessing, and goes, with no word said.

But at night a voice comes on the wind, a phantom
Torments me, touching my ageing limbs with fire:
A sea boy out of Smyrna. Two years we lived
In unlawful love, thieving and drinking together,
Till he left me for a wealthy Lebanese
For a new overcoat and a villa in Cairo.

With mouth of pomegranate, with skin of jessamine,
With eyes like wintry flowers, with cheeks firm as olives,
With corrupt blood, with the treachery of a panther.
Two years we lived at loggerheads together.
In his flesh I embraced the flesh of the young Hyakinthos.
And between midnight and morning he taunts me still.

Jack the Swagger's Song

'Damn this dry shingle country,'
Old Jack the Swagger cried –
'The rutting hare beneath; above
The brown hawk in his pride;
And not one green gooseberry bush
To suck and lay beside.

'Beyond the Rock and Pillar
One day when I was young
I plucked a berry from the bush
And laid it on my tongue:
No sourer, wilder, gladder fruit
From the grey schist rock sprung.

'Ten feet below the creekbed
Those buried waters lie,
And had I but one billy full
I'd mock the raging sky –
But crazy in the heat mirage
Like any beast I'll die;

'And when the squatter hears it
At most he'll thumb his reins
And say, "Bad Luck!" – and soon the creek
(From an icefield it drains)
Headhigh will soak my shirt and run
Aflood in my dry veins.'

Elegy at the Year's End

At the year's end I come to my father's house
Where passion fruit hang gold above an open doorway
And garden trees bend to the visiting bird:
   Here first the single vision
Entered my heart, as to a dusty room
Enters the pure tyrannical wind of heaven.

The coal burns out; the quiet ash remains
That tired minds and coarsened bodies know.
   Small town of corrugated iron roofs
Between the low volcanic saddle
And offshore reef where blue cod browse,
From husks of exile, humbled, I come to your fond prison.

At an elder uncle's deathbed I read the graph
Of suffering in the face of country cousins.
   These have endured what men hold in common,
The cross of custom, the marriage bed of knives;
Their angular faces reflecting his
Whose body lies stiff under the coverlet.

One may walk again to the fisherman's rock, hearing
The long waves tumble, from America riding
Where mottled kelpbeds heave to a pale sun,
   But not again see green Aphrodite
Rise to transfigure the noon. Rather the Sophoclean
Chorus: *All shall be taken.*

Or by the brown lagoon stand idle
Where to their haunted coves the safe flocks go,
And envy the paradise drake his brilliant sexual plumage.

For single vision dies. Spirit and flesh are sundered
In the kingdom of no love. Our stunted passions bend
To serve again familiar social devils.

Brief is the visiting angel. In corridors of hunger
Our lives entwined suffer the common ill:
Living and dying, breathing and begetting.
Meanwhile on maimed gravestones under the towering fennel
Moves the bright lizard, sunloved, basking in
    The moment of animal joy.

Lament for Barney Flanagan
Licensee of the Hesperus Hotel

Flanagan got up on a Saturday morning,
Pulled on his pants while the coffee was warming:
He didn't remember the doctor's warning,
    'Your heart's too big, Mr Flanagan.'

Barney Flanagan, sprung like a frog
From a wet root in an Irish bog –
May his soul escape from the tooth of the dog!
    God have mercy on Flanagan.

Barney Flanagan R.I.P.
Rode to his grave on Hennessy's
Like a bottle-cork boat in the Irish Sea.
    The bell-boy rings for Flanagan.

Barney Flanagan, ripe for a coffin,
Eighteen stone and brandy-rotten,
Patted the housemaid's velvet bottom –
    'Oh, is it you, Mr Flanagan?'

The sky was bright as a new milk token.
Bill the Bookie and Shellshock Hogan
Waited outside for the pub to open –
 'Good day, Mr Flanagan.'

At noon he was drinking in the lounge bar corner
With a sergeant of police and a racehorse owner
When the Angel of Death looked over his shoulder –
 'Could you spare a moment, Flanagan?'

Oh the deck was cut; the bets were laid;
But the very last card that Barney played
Was the Deadman's Trump, the bullet of Spades –
 'Would you like more air, Mr Flanagan?'

The priest came running but the priest came late
For Barney was banging at the Pearly Gate.
St Peter said, 'Quiet! You'll have to wait
 For a hundred masses, Flanagan.'

The regular boys and the loud accountants
Left their nips and their seven-ounces
As chickens fly when the buzzard pounces –
 'Have you heard about old Flanagan?'

Cold in the parlour Flanagan lay
Like a bride at the end of her marriage day.
The Waterside Workers' Band will play
 A brass goodbye to Flanagan.

While publicans drink their profits still,
While lawyers flock to be in at the kill,
While Aussie barmen milk the till
 We will remember Flanagan.

For Barney had a send-off and no mistake.
He died like a man for his country's sake;
And the Governor-General came to his wake.
    Drink again to Flanagan!

Despise not, O Lord, the work of Thine own hands
And let light perpetual shine upon him.

Letter to Australia

The images of natural joy
Perturb my winter as I stretch
An arm to soothe the mongrel bitch
Conscience who shares a cellar with me,
And shout across the blinding Tasman
What must come thinly, cold and queer,
Above the wry surf-pounded year
From my bone house to yours, Chapman.

The mirrors of confounding joy
Blaze from the natural world to mine,
Much sunlight on a little pain
That will go with me when I go;
And in the cave of memory
Ring always the salt siren voices
Proclaiming to the flesh that dies
Original breath and entity.

You, friend, have seen and wondered at
The rose that opens like a wound
Where our blood upon the ground
Denies the existential night:

My friend, I have not seen another
Cause for joy, so rest
My head upon the cancered breast
Of Cybele who is the dream's mother.

Pride's counsel; but the true Church
Foreseeing that a Christian mind
More than pagan is inclined
To lie down deaf in the last ditch,
Rivets home what the world lacks,
Love's iron contiguity:
Her mills of domesticity
Grind small until the grain cracks.

Certainly those who chased the dream,
A jack-o'-lantern in a field,
Have either caught their death's cold
Or come with muddy breeches home.
And yet our torment does not close
When doctors put the dream to sleep.
Body cries for the soul's scope,
Soul desires the body's peace.

The canticle of natural joy
Always outside my rackrent house
Tells me that I was born to praise.
The pears have fallen from the tree;
The wasps have fed. Remember
My voice a while in Canberra.
So, if at all, the heart is nourished.

The dark blue Tasman heaving
Writes on a beach of scars
That freedom has another meaning
Beyond our years and powers.

[47]

The Woman on the Stair

'Come in, my dear; you're very late,'
   Said the woman on the stair.
'Take off that muddy overcoat
And I'll . . . why is your face so white?'
'The night frost is hard,' he said,
   'There's winter in the air.'

'I'll get a drop of brandy then,'
   Said the woman on the stair,
'And cushions so we both can lean
At the sitting-room fire; but kiss me, John!'
'My mouth would leave a mark,' he said,
   'And blood upon your hair.'

'This is a silly game to play,'
   Said the woman on the stair.
'I told you only yesterday
That he would spend tonight away . . .'
'Don't touch my heart,' he said,
   'The knife slits deepest there.'

'Then, go – if you are what you are,'
   Said the woman on the stair.
'To a live man I gave my heart,
Let the dead lie in their own dark!'
'Oh I have bought hell's cold,' he said,
   'And you the cost must share.'

Heard in a Sod Chimney

'What eye could wish for more,'
   Sings the first voice in the wind,
'Than yellow spume on the seashore,
Glitter of breakers boiling,
And a girl wading there
Whom the hard light strips,
Breast and hips, grey eyes, and brindled hair
A nest of young snakes coiling?'

'Ah, no such countenance,'
   Sings the second voice in the wind,
'But the town girl at a country dance
A swan among geese sailing
(How they cackle and hiss!) –
Her high heels clattering go
To and fro: no farmer's son dare kiss
That proud mouth at the frostwhite railing.'

'How bright the marsh fires burn!'
   Sings the third voice in the wind.
'I have blown over many a cairn
And bone to bone spieling
Had heavy tales to tell
How this one, that one, fair
In the world's air drew breath and glimmered well
Who now stares blind at a marble ceiling.'

The Fisherman

Between the day and evening
I fish from Barney's rock,

And watch the weedy channels fill
And hear the small waves knock,
And feel below their ledge's roof
The tugging greenbone flock.

When spiring seabirds mingle
Between the wave and sky,
The ka'wai chase the herrings in
Like soldiers dressed to die,
And on the beach for hands to pick
In flapping shoals they lie.

Upon an army pension
It suits a single man
To take from the sea's full cupboard
Whatever food he can.
The wound I got at Passchendaele
Throbs with the dying sun.

While loud across the sandhills
Clangs out the Sunday bell
I drop my line and sinker down
Through the weed-fronded swell,
And what I see there after dark
Let the blind wave tell.

Crossing Cook Strait

The night was clear, sea calm; I came on deck
To stretch my legs, find perhaps
Gossip, a girl in green slacks at the rail
Or just the logline feathering a dumb wake.

The ship swung in the elbow of the Strait.
'Dolphins!' I cried – 'let the true sad Venus
Rise riding her shoals, teach me as once to wonder
And wander at ease, be glad and never regret.'

But night increased under the signal stars.
In the dark bows, facing the flat sea,
Stood one I had not expected, yet knew without surprise
As the Janus made formidable by loveless years.

His coat military; his gesture mild –
'Well met,' he said, 'on the terrestrial journey
From chaos into light – what light it is
Contains our peril and purpose, history has not revealed.'

'Sir – ', I began. He spoke with words of steel –
'I am Seddon and Savage, the socialist father.
You have known me only in my mask of Dionysus
Amputated in bar rooms, dismembered among wheels.

'I woke in my civil tomb hearing a shout
For bread and justice. It was not here.
That sound came thinly over the waves from China;
Stones piled on my grave had all but shut it out.

'I walked forth gladly to find the angry poor
Who are my nation; discovered instead
The glutton seagulls squabbling over crusts
And policies made and broken behind locked doors.

'I have watched the poets also at their trade.
I have seen them burning with a wormwood brilliance.
Love was the one thing lacking on their page,
The crushed herb of grief at another's pain.

[51]

'Your civil calm breeds inward poverty
That chafes for change. The ghost of Adam
Gibbering demoniac in drawing-rooms
Will drink down hemlock with his sugared tea.

'You feed your paupers concrete. They work well.
Ask for no second meal, vote, pay tribute
Of silence on Anzac Day in the pub urinal;
Expose death only by a mushroom smell.

'My counsel was naïve. Anger is bread
To the poor, their guns more accurate than justice.
Because their love has not decayed to a wintry fungus
And hope to the wish for power among the dead.

'In Kaitangata the miner's falling sweat
Wakes in the coal seam fossil flowers.
The clerk puts down his pen and takes his coat;
He will not be back today or the next day either.'

With an ambiguous salute he left me.
The ship moved into a stronger sea,
Bludgeoned alive by the rough mystery
Of love in the running straits of history.

A Rope for Harry Fat

Oh some have killed in angry love
    And some have killed in hate,
And some have killed in foreign lands
    To serve the business State.
The hangman's hands are abstract hands
    Though sudden death they bring –

'The hangman keeps our country pure,'
  Says Harry Fat the King.

Young love will kick the chairs about
  And like a rush fire burn,
Desiring what it cannot have,
  A true love in return.
Who knows what rage and darkness fall
  When lovers' thoughts grow cold?
'Whoever kills must pay the price,'
  Says Harry Fat the old.

With violent hands a young man tries
  To mend the shape of life.
This one used a shotgun
  And that one used a knife.
And who can see the issues plain
  That vex our groaning dust?
'The Law is greater than the man,'
  Says Harry Fat the just.

Te Whiu was too young to vote,
  The prison records show.
Some thought he was too young to hang;
  Legality said, *No.*
Who knows what fear the raupo hides
  Or where the wild duck flies?
'A trapdoor and a rope is best,'
  Says Harry Fat the wise.

Though many a time he rolled his coat
  And on the bare boards lay,
He lies in heavy concrete now
  Until the Reckoning Day.

[53]

In linen sheet or granite aisle
    Sleep Ministers of State.
'We cannot help the idle poor,'
    Says Harry Fat the great.

Mercy stirred like a summer wind
    The wigs and polished boots
And the long Jehovah faces
    Above their Sunday suits.
The jury was uncertain;
    The judge debated long.
'Let justice take her rightful course,'
    Said Harry Fat the strong.

The butcher boy and baker boy
    Were whistling in the street
When the hangman bound Te Whiu's eyes
    And strapped his hands and feet,
Who stole to buy a bicycle
    And killed in panic blood.
'The parson won his soul at length,'
    Said Harry Fat the good.

Oh some will kill in rage and fear
    And some will kill in hate,
And some will kill in foreign lands
    To serve the master State.
Justice walks heavy in the land;
    She bears a rope and shroud.
'We will not change our policy,'
    Says Harry Fat the proud.

In fires of no return

While bluegum fables burn
To summer's ash
In fires of no return
Above the farms and crying folds
That house the doom of flesh,
To Barney's pulpit rock I climb
Where the sea aisles burn cold
In fires of no return
And maned breakers praise
The death hour of the sun.
To wave and bird I open wide
The bible of my rimrock days,
To salt-grey ngaio boughs that cross
The forehead of the west,
To Venus' holy star who smiles
Upon the lives she cannot save,
Man, beast, bird, lover
In orchards of a spring desire,
Hermit old on his wintry pyre,
All flesh wound in the bright snare,
In fires of no return
Wrung by the power of the prince of the air.

My country fathers laid
Under angel and cold urn
In fields of silence burn,
From folds of ngaio and strong fern
Turn their immortal eyes on mine,
Tell me this day the world was made.
I hear in frond and shell
The voice of the drowned sailor
Tossed on the black bar, with a winy breath

Shout from the feast of Cana.
How love has raked the embers of his death.
And hermit from a holy cell
I watch my brother
King shag dive
Down from his windy
Rock to the humble tide
Where the sea poor, old crab and limpet,
Sigh to the resurrection thunder.
Among night dunes the moony lovers
In lupin shade far and near
Twined under Venus' carnal star
Mock the power of the prince of the air.
Their doomed flesh answers an undying summer.

By the Dry Cardrona

I can tell where cherries grow
    By the dry Cardrona,
Where I plucked them long ago
    On a day when I was sober.

My father wore a parson's coat
    By the dry Cardrona;
He kept a tally of the sheep and the goats,
    And I was never sober.

My mother sewed her Sunday skirt
    By the dry Cardrona,
They said she died of a broken heart
    For I was never sober.

O lay my bones till the judgement crack
    By the wild Cardrona!
The blanket swag upon my back
    Will pillow me drunk or sober.

I loved a girl and only one
    By the dry Cardrona,
She owned a stable and a scheelite mine
    But I was never sober.

All rivers run to the rimless grave,
    Even the wild Cardrona,
But the black cherry bent my way
    One day when I was sober.

At Hokianga

Green floating mangrove pods reveal,
Plucked from the lagging tide, their small
Man-in-a-boat, kernel and clitoris:
Set free to sail, they climb a hundred beaches,
Germinate in night-black mud. Tell,
Historian, how the broken tribes were healed
In a land of exhausted wells, north
From that great ragged capital
Flung like a coat to rot on garden earth.

In houses thatched with nikau palm,
Fearing the dead, riding bareback
On hill stallions, those who learned before us
The secret of survival, to be patient,
Suffer, and shut no doors,
Change all things to their habit, bridge

The bogs with branch laid to branch:
Nourished at compliant breasts, wish only
To drink with friends, own a launch.

To scrape the bones of the dead, how needful.
Lest they should walk, undo forgetfulness
With blight on crops, sickness at home.
In packed ground the missionary fathers
Drowned at river crossings, rest in one bed,
While a boy cuts from flax a spirit boat
Perfect, lightly as a bird's wing
Riding the void of waters
Untaught, a full hour floating.

Pyrrha

As kites rise up against the wind
Out of the past I summon Pyrrha,
Girl of plaited wheat, first
Mentor of love revealed in dying.

She has come back with a burning-glass
To whom once my thoughts clung
Like branches under weirs tumbling:
That freedom led to the lion's jaws,
A mind riddled by illusion.
The autumn sky is hers, a flooding
Trick of light on bars of broken cloud.

The streetlamp tells me where she lived.
Re-entering that square, untidy room
Where cups lie mixed with finger-bones
I find her again. Forehead too full,

Opaque blue eyes, bruised archaic smile
Dug from under shards. Pleasure,
A crab gripping the spine;
A mouth lent, not given;
Hair like marram grass, that made
On the short sofa, a burglar's tent.

Rib from my side, Pyrrha,
I who was young am older,
The wound healed, the flask of seed dry
You cried once, 'I am drifting, drifting.'
Self-pitying, too often drunk,
I did not see your need of comforting.
Pestle and mortar pounded us
Early to a dry volcanic dust.

Green Figs at Table

'To eat a green fig, my dear,
Torn from the belly of unreason,
Honey white or brown when you open it,
The female parts, a story, or a poem –'
    'Perhaps.'

'The taste sticks in one's mouth. Even now
Barometer wounds begin to throb, simply
Because you are a woman, woman in her rubbed flesh
Dressed for carnage – ' 'I thought there was
    A better name for it.'

'Action. Society as undertaker
Measures us for coffins, plugs up the orifices
By which pleasure might enter or pity escape

Mothers admire the handsome corpse.
   That cost so little

'To be tidied. They cover the rope mark on the throat.'
'You were talking of figs –' 'Yes, figs.
I would like to be, at length, Odysseus lounging
With loaf and wine-cup in the shade
   Of his daughter the bent olive,

'But I too roast in the brass bull
Of conscience, remembering at this autumn table
Woman ganched in cupboards of the mind or
Geometrical on the black glaze of an urn –'
   'I burn in waiting

'For the sea to rise or the god to descend
And hear, in coffee shops, the mill of gossip turning.'
'Blood runs from my nail into the soya dish;
Oil boats rust, chained at darkened wharves.
   One movement could shake

'Us free, I think –' 'One should not say too much.
Enter, without knocking, the door of the fig.'

At Akitio

Consider this barbarian coast,
Traveller, you who have lost
Lover or friend. It has never made
Anything out of anything.
Drink at these bitter springs.

Fishing at river mouth, a woman
Uses the sea-drilled stone her mother used
For sinker, as big kahawai come,
As tides press upward to time's source.
This coast is shelter to the shearing gangs
Who burn dead matai in their kitchen.

Squirearch, straight-backed rider, built
An ethos of the leisured life,
Lawn, antlered hall and billiard room,
Glass candelabra brought from Paris,
The homestead foundered among fields.
Unhorsed they sleep.

A girl with a necklace of mako teeth
They dug from a sandcliff facing south,
Axe and broken needle.
Stay good under slab and cross
Thin bones of children burnt by cholera,
Made tidy by the last strict nurse.
As tributary of a greater stream
Your single grief enlarges now
The voice of night in kumara gardens,
Prayer of the bush pigeon.

One drowned at the cattle crossing,
One tossed and kicked by a bucking horse –
Who died without confession, wanting
No wafer in their teeth –
Does the toetoe plume their altar?
Are they held safe in the sea's grail?
This gullied mounded earth, tonned
With silence, and the sun's gaze
On a choir of breakers, has outgrown

[61]

The pain of love. Drink,
Traveller, at these pure springs.

Remember, though, the early strength
Of bull-voiced water when the boom broke
And eels clung to the banks, logs
Plunged and pierced the river hymen.
Remember iron-coloured skulls
Of cattle thrown to the crab's crypt,
Driftwood piled by river flood
On the long beach, battered limb
And loin where the red-backed spider breeds,
By a halcyon sea the shapes of man,
Emblems of our short fever.

Pluck then from ledges of the sea
Crayfish for the sack. Not now but later
Think what you were born for. Drink,
Child, at the springs of sleep.

Howrah Bridge
(to my wife)

Taller than the stair of Qtub Minar
These iron beams oppress the eagle's town.
Bare heels will dint them slowly.
And swollen Gunga's muscles move
Beneath, with freight of garbage,
Oar and sail, the loot of many lives.

In the unsleeping night my thoughts
Are millet falling from an iron pan,
While you, my dear, in Delhi lying down

[62]

Enter the same room by another door.
The rupee god has trampled here;
The poor implore a Marxist cage.
Dragon seed, the huddled bundles lying
In doorways have perhaps one chilli,
A handful of ground maize.
King Famine rules. Tout and owl-eyed whore
Whose talons pluck and stain the sleeve,
Angels of judgement, husk the soul
Till pity, pity only stays.

Out of my wounds they have made stars:
Each is an eye that looks on you.

School Days

I touch them with a word, so close they stand
After a thousand hours and days,
Older than Cocteau, in the dream museum
Of corridors and changing rooms:
A palace, jail and maze.

There I imbibed, as at a breast, truth
Beside the simple streams and elms;
England, my wet nurse, with her bitter milk.
So from sugared childhood came
On to the watershed of tears
With those small angular companions,
Handlers of the penis and the pen.

Hard to forgive them even now,
Precursors of the adult nightmare –
Franey, Nero of the dormitory,

Holmes, with the habits of a jaguar
And the sleek animal hide,
Waiting in a bend of the high stone stair.

Plunged early into the abyss of life
Where the tormentors move,
At war with God, the terrible Watcher,
An octopus behind a round glass window
With knives and justice, but no love.

That guilt grew wrongly, driven underground
With the first prickings of raw sense.
Yet there was friendship, comics, dominoes,
A dried newt like a bootsole in a drain,
New conkers like peeled testicles,
Sharing of exile, and the habit, pain.

The village like a mother stayed outside
With wells and horses, till the coat
Of manhood could be stitched and worn –
And the green mandrake Poetry
Born whole and shrieking one bleak night
Under stiff sheets and wincing at the dawn.

Eioko

That one should suffer for a nation,
Small folded hands, blackcurrant eyes
Alive with character among the sequins:
Eioko, sold in Choshi by her father
(Leg sores and all) for thirty thousand yen,
As if with stakes of split bamboo
To bank one paddy field against the river.

Her templebones pierced for the blood to flow
Lest she should die untimely
(By God transfusèd thence to graceless souls)
Eight days head down above a charcoal pit . . .
For Eioko, a deadlier martyrdom,
At drunken midnight tables
Displayed like butcher's meat, unable
To yawn at will, or smoke or frown or sit,

Becomes a stupid mask, an aching cistern.

The granite maxim: One must always please
Tourist, soldier, ape and boor,
With courtesy more durable than love.
Great dolls like captives nod above her bed.
In Tokyo's ashy dawn she gently touches
A chopstick-holder carved like a green fish,
Sharing her rice bowl with a child more poor.

At the Tomb of Theseus

Bramble and couchgrass twine above
The tumulus of giant bones.
This king despised his mother's love,
Subdued bullheaded chaos, built
An aqueduct, a cenotaph.
His bones rot like other bones.
Human hatred, human guilt,
Fuel the engine of the State.
The legless beggar at the gate
Has freedom still to spit and laugh.
The twining couchgrass seeds above
Bones that were ignorant of love.

Be Happy in Bed

One landscape, many women:
Ambition of that savage empty boy
Haunting the bathing sheds and diamond bay,
Composing verses in an upstairs room.
Now the long windings of a broken sense
In humorous elegiacs write his doom.

Boathouses on the edge of Nowhere
Recur to trouble after-dinner sleep,
White legs among the cords and rowlocks –
'There is a spirit in the moving water
Forgives and understands us
Though God has gone inside and slammed the door.'
Where the boats ride endlessly
Grip and hold the sea king's daughter.

Sex taught him sadness: like St Lawrence
Roasting on the grid of conscience:
'One side is brown; now try the other.'
The self so persecuted by enigmas
Prefers a mountain to a nagging mother.

Put off the past: you have endured it,
Enjoyed, or else confessed it.
This luxury like cut veins in a bath
Stains too much the moving water.
No meaning now in that direction
Though skeletons toward the salt pans creep.
The age of sex, the age of centaurs
Returns to punish after-dinner sleep.

Mandrakes for Supper

Memory feeds us on a prison diet
Of bits and scraps. 'Remember Mr X –,
That simple solemn man, so deathly quiet;

'And Sally Z –, compounded of raw sex
And circumstance' – 'Ah yes, her corn-gold hair . . .'
A land where roams Tyrannosaurus Rex,

The giant lizard, calloused by despair –
In Nowhere I received my education
(If memory can be trusted) mooching there

Like Dante's ghost, among a faceless nation.
The white antarctic Gorgon was my mentor:
Her cloudy arms, her eyes of desolation

Sisterly gazing from the whirlwind's centre,
Received, embraced my naked intuition.
The town of Nilburg too I shrank to enter

(If memory serves me right) and wept contrition
For indistinct all-but-committed crimes
In gelding-rooms and caves of parturition.

Yet undeniably I laughed at times
With those who shared my headless hullaballoo:
Fogeaters, Dwarfs, Green Quims and Paradigms.

Cellars of Nilburg! how I hated you,
Your Ixion wheels, hot frogs and icy toads,
Your existential climate where I grew

Into an adult mandrake. (Memory loads
My plate with mushrooms.) But I woke at length
And left you, travelling light by mountain roads
To Elsewhere; drank at desert wells; gained strength.

Elephanta

Accordion and sweet brisk drum
Waken a lounging passion

Outside the wooden teashop where a young
Black-trousered androgynous dancer

Trounces the dust, crooking a maggot's finger,
While pockmarked queers applaud and smoke.

Great hawks like monoplanes
Above the bony tamarind,

Above the quarried rock sail high, high,
And Shiva like a business uncle watches

The village girls with cans to fill
File through the temple to a covered cistern.

Consider. Seasnake, white cloud minnow,
Octopus and moray eel,

Lovely in their lit aquariums
Breathe water as we do,

Have the advantage that they cannot feel.
Yet I have seen, across an angry tide-rip,

The narrow coffin-boat, the catamaran,
Go simply as a girl, with forward-leaning

Mast and torn triangular sail,
Leaving a crowded net behind.

Sisyphus

Sisyphus, unhappy one,
Mechanic of an old fraternity,
To whom the simple and unchanging
Processes of day and night
Seem but a cage, a treadmill motion –
In your glass castle over
The city looms and furnaces,
With an enamelled mistress
And rugs to deaden sound –
The hour, the heavy boulder
On which you lean your clay cold shoulder
Cannot tell you how to weep,
Cannot set ajar the iron gate.

Wilderness is wilderness
Though the skysigns talk of love.
King of the silver mountain,
The deepest tunnel leads you down
To a torn and blinded mirror
And the angers of the tomb.
Take then, baldhead, if you must,
The pearl revolver from your desk,
But throw one look before you go
Across the unbought harbour
Rising with its freight of air and snow

[69]

Look on the earthly presences,
The unrewarded silences.

A Prospect of Old Age

Suppose a nest of bees, their honey staining
Brown brittle paper on the wall:
A sun dried hut of bricks, bone-dry
Kiln for the hermit years remaining.

Let this man work entirely to recapture
The aerial music of his youth,
Or talk with angels as the carnal
Agony subsides. A stony rapture

This would be. Revengeful, as if joking,
Cheat Caesar by apparent death,
Deny his relatives their pound of flesh,
To criticise his smell, his cough, his smoking.

Let that sweet corrosive dream
More dangerous than Simeon Stylites'
Take shape: an old man at his prayers,
Self-gutted, tugged from the human stream,

An old grey gander with no goose
Who wakes in moonlight groaning for
The dead to answer. Hears above his head
The cranky shutter clatter loose.

Footnote to Antony and Cleopatra

How did the balance come about?
I do not think the critics know.
Freud and Bradley cramp our thumbs
That try to bend Ulysses' bow.

Was it red-haired Elizabeth
Who smiled on poets like a star?
I do not think the answer lies
In any civic calendar.

That dark mysterious gentleman
In Stratford rents a dusty room.
Ape and jackdaw brag above
The strong Egyptian harlot's tomb,

And I, on thinner gruel fed,
Envy his autumn discontent
Who took the fecund Nile to bed
And left a world as monument.

Ballad of Calvary Street

On Calvary Street are trellises
Where bright as blood the roses bloom,
And gnomes like pagan fetishes
Hang their hats on an empty tomb
Where two old souls go slowly mad,
National Mum and Labour Dad.

Each Saturday when full of smiles
The children come to pay their due,

Mum takes down the family files
And cover to cover she thumbs them through,
Poor Len before he went away
And Mabel on her wedding day.

The meal-brown scones display her knack,
Her polished oven spits with rage,
While in Grunt Grotto at the back
Dad sits and reads the Sporting Page,
Then ambles out in boots of lead
To weed around the parsnip bed.

A giant parsnip sparks his eye,
Majestic as the Tree of Life;
He washes it and rubs it dry
And takes it in to his old wife –
'Look Laura, would that be a fit?
The bastard has a flange on it!'

When both were young she would have laughed,
A goddess in her tartan skirt,
But wisdom, age and mothercraft
Have rubbed it home that men like dirt:
Five children and a fallen womb,
A golden crown beyond the tomb.

Nearer the bone, sin is sin,
And women bear the cross of woe,
And that affair with Mrs Flynn
(It happened thirty years ago)
Though never mentioned, means that he
Will get no sugar in his tea.

The afternoon goes by, goes by,
The angels harp above a cloud;
A son-in-law with spotted tie
And daughter Alice fat and loud
Discuss the virtues of insurance
And stuff their tripes with trained endurance.

Flood-waters hurl upon the dyke
And Dad himself can go to town,
For little Charlie on his trike
Has ploughed another iris down.
His parents rise to chain the beast,
Brush off the last crumbs of their lovefeast.

And so these two old fools are left,
A rosy pair in evening light,
To question Heaven's dubious gift,
To hag and grumble, growl and fight:
The love they kill won't let them rest,
Two birds that peck in one fouled nest.

Why hammer nails? Why give no change?
Habit, habit clogs them dumb.
The Sacred Heart above the range
Will bleed and burn till Kingdom Come,
But Yin and Yang won't ever meet
In Calvary Street, in Calvary Street.

Evidence at the Witch Trials

No woman's pleasure did I feel
     Under the hazel tree
When heavy as a sack of meal

The Black Man mounted me,
But cold as water from a dyke
   His seed that quickened me.

What his age I cannot tell;
   Foul he was, and fair.
There blew between us both from Hell
   A blast of grit and fire,
And like a boulder is the babe
   That in my womb I bear.

Though I was youngest in that band
   Yet I was quick to learn.
A red dress he promised me
   And red the torches burn.
Between the faggot and the flame
   I see his face return.

Christchurch 1948

The true town will evade your map,
Murderous, choked by its cathedral stone.
Those granite jowls I remember,
A.'s hornet nest of Yeatsian prose,
D. flattened in a chair, dead drunk on gin,
A vague fog rising from the Avon,
A city founded in wanhope
And English, English, English to the bone.

Hunger for light sustained me there
Under the sign of Dionysus-Hades,
In a kennel with a torn gas mantle,
Alive on milk and benzedrine,

Haruspex, probing the flight of birds.
Once came an old man with a rotting face,
And more than once my girl, to squeeze
Kisses out, cool whey from curds.

The founding father in his stovepipe hat
Watched, but could not understand
My rage, her sweet potato beauty.
The bells implored us to die soon.
Sickles of foam on winter beaches
In their angelic speech instructed
Two children sighing in the labyrinth
For light, for the country of high noon.

Obsequy for Dylan Thomas

A gallon of gin and a flitch of pork,
Thomas lies slug-a-bed in New York.
Flat on her back in the big whorehouse
The English Language mourns her spouse.
She weeps as she works and keeps the tally
He won't bowl home from Dead Man's Alley.
He drinks with the Great Bear and the Plough.
    The short-stitch tailors,
    The coffin-nailers,
The bedlam jailors
              have her now.

Winter

Winter unbundles a sack of storms
Above the flat scrub country.

Far at sea a trawling captain
Watches a double rainbow arching,
Noah's good sign, along the black horizon,
Hopes for groper, fat cod, terakihi.

A bureaucrat lights the gas fire
That warms his raw-edged afternoon,
Plucks a folder from a grey steel file,
Coughs, and eyes the telephone.

A housewife sees her washing, three-days-wet.
Hang draggled in the tugging wind,
Measures the old chair for new covers,
An ache of winter in the mind.

A child dawdling home from school
Builds little twig dams in the gutter,
Sings to himself although his shoes
Are damp, and bullies lurk at Butcher's Corner.

Winter unwraps a parcel of stones
For old and sick and sad, and homeless walkers.

To Jacquie
(a dedication)

Statesman, prophet, dancer,
On their high tightrope walk.
A few fire-hardened verses
Shaped by a tomahawk
May help in an hour of storm
To hold the great tent firm.

And if it should blow over
As it has done before,
Let us go and plant together
A hedge of sycamore.
That windy scent will rise and grow
Beyond the fire, beyond the snow.

Makara Beach

Rock pudenda thrust into the sea
From that grey ledge below the valley's apron,
Some scattering-place of souls
Where they go out on the landless water.
While the grandmother sea spun sheets of lace
My wife and kids and I came there,
Threw stones, ate cold ice-cream.
I watched the wind sabre the water face,

Not long out of the grog mill, griping,
Wanting a vision of the Damascus kind,
Explosion of light. It was all there,
Hidden in that ash-pit place,
Sweet rage of water, stone or wood
Or wave-dismantled shell. I rediscover
The uncreated music, probing now
The bones of rock, the body of my lover.

Brown child, waif of time, you are the lens
By which the sky and earth unlock
Their hidden light for me. Boat and bach,
The shingle creek of sliding waves
Where boys gaff giant eels,
Great-uddered cows below the toetoe plumes,

These are the simple Eden of desire
Your substance to my soul reveals.

On the Death of her Body

It is a thought breaking the granite heart
Time has given me, that my one treasure,
Your limbs, those passion-vines, that bamboo body

Should age and slacken, rot
Some day in a ghastly clay-stopped hole.
They led me to the mountains beyond pleasure

Where each is not gross body or blank soul
But a strong harp the wind of genesis
Makes music in, such resonant music

That I was Adam, loosened by your kiss
From time's hard bond, and you,
My love, in the world's first summer stood

Plucking the flowers of the abyss.

Election 1960

Hot sun. Lizards frolic
Fly-catching on the black ash

That was green rubbish. Tiny dragons,
They dodge among the burnt broom stems

As if the earth belonged to them
Without condition. In the polling booths

A democratic people have elected
King Log, King Stork, King Log, King Stork again.

Because I like a wide and silent pond
I voted Log. That party was defeated.

Now frogs will dive and scuttle to avoid
That poking idiot bill, the iron gullet:

Delinquent frogs! Stork is an active King,
A bird of principle, benevolent,

And Log is Log, an old time-serving post
Hacked from a totara when the land was young.

The Sixties
(for Louis Johnson)

'The icy dawn of the sixties' –
Yes, you have it there.
Today I saw a black sperm whale
Rolled on the rocks at Pukerua Bay.

The stench grew loud as I came near,
Gulls were grabbing at the kill.
From that sleek projectile body
Jutted a gigantic reddened phallus
Mauled by the Cook Strait squid.

Under the sunset fires it seemed to be
The body of our common love
That bedrooms, bar rooms never killed,
The natural power behind our acts and verses
Murdered by triviality.

[79]

Ballad of John Silent

To Babylon town
At morning I came
Looking for someone
To tell me my name,

From brown hills and wide water,
From my father's garden,
From my brother's joking,
From my mother's kitchen,

Ignorant and early
And not very big,
With my soul inside me
Like a ferret in a bag.

Men with money,
Men with books,
Followed me with monkeys
Riding on their backs,

Chattering, 'Listen, boy,
Make it a deal!
You can have the whole town
For your brand new soul.'

'Tell me my name then.'
'We don't know.'
They frowned and they threatened
But I went by,

Past the hospital gate
And the railway line,

Past the Grand Hotel
And the church so fine,

To a house where a woman
Was leaning on a door
With eyes like the sunset
And a flower in her hair.

'Lady, can you tell me
My own true name?'
'Yes, John Silent –
Come in, John.'

On a big brass bed
I laid her down.
Out of the bag
The ferret sprang,

Quicker than I say it
Out through the keyhole
Wriggled and vanished
My red-eyed soul.

'Do you love me, John?'
'Why, yes, I do.'
'Then sing me a song
While I play with you.'

'I can sing no song
When my soul is gone.'
'Then tell me a story,
Silent John.'

'To Babylon town
At daybreak I came
Looking for someone
To tell me my name,

'From sour hills and wild water,
From my father's truncheon,
From my brother's envy,
From my mother's bitching

'And lucky I found
A woman for a blacksmith
To forge me the fetters
I go to my death with.'

Brown Bone

Bone in the river bed,
Old bone like a honeycomb,
Brown bone, man bone,
Where do you come from?

I camped on a shingle flat
Beside the loud Rakaia,
And drove my tent pegs in
And built a fire of dry manuka.

I'd bread in the saddlebags
And tea in the black billy
And enough tobacco to last me
All the way to Gabriel's Gully.

I stretched out like a log
Dreaming of girls and cider,

And Death came like a riding man
With hooves of mountain water.

Bone in the river bed,
Old bone cracked by the sun,
Brown bone like a honeycomb,
Don't take it hard, man.

Brighton

Glass-fronted baches stand and look
On the brown hurdling waves

That die at a brackish river mouth
Choked by the sand at every tide.

A township full of ears! They used to send
A springcart round the sandhills to bring in

The drunken elders. Toetoe, marram grass,
Teach nothing to the narrow church of tin.

Beyond the high-banked green domain
Where boy and girl lying in lupin mazes

Pluck the dragon's apple, older now,
I go on beaches when the tide is low

And fish for poems where my four dead uncles,
Jack, Billy, Mark and Sandy,

Let down their lines from laps of broken stone
For the fat red cod and small-mouthed greenbone.

At Taieri Mouth

Flax-pods unload their pollen
Above the steel-bright cauldron

Of Taieri, the old water-dragon
Sliding out from a stone gullet

Below the Maori-ground. Scrub horses
Come down at night to smash the fences

Of the whaler's children. Trypots have rusted
Leaving the oil of anger in the blood

Of those who live in two-roomed houses
Mending nets or watching from a window

The great south sky fill up with curdled snow.
Their cows eat kelp along the beaches.

The purple sailor drowned in thighboots
Drifting where the currents go

Cannot see the flame some girl has lighted
In a glass chimney, but in five days' time

With bladder-weed around his throat
Will ride the drunken breakers in.

Ballade of the Happy Bureaucrat

Quite often when I'm feeling low
    I like to take a purgative
(My neighbours looking through the window
    Are damnably inquisitive);
    I hope my readers will forgive
If I've omitted this or that
    From the tenor of my narrative
Because I am a bureaucrat.

At eight o'clock to work I go
    And on the train I'm talkative;
I lay my pencils in a row
    With the infallible objective
    Of opening out a new perspective;
I wear a very nice grey hat
    And keep my brain and body active
Because I am a bureaucrat.

Please don't suppose I'm ignorant though
    Of the Negative Affirmative;
I learnt it quite a while ago
    And chant it when I'm feeling pensive.
    My nature's very sensitive,
I should have been an acrobat;
    My values are all relative
Because I am a bureaucrat.

My feelings were contemplative
    On the day that the Commission sat,
And I can glide through any sieve
    Because I am a bureaucrat.

Bushed

Bush country. The tree spiders build
Their houses to the east, where the sun can enter

Gossamer tunnels. Also
Grass flows to the north, bent over

By southerly winds. A man from Te Kuiti
Told me this, lest I should be caught

Without a compass in bush country
And walk in circles through the blinding hills

Filthy, foodless, frantic, lame,
Mocked by the bellbird's requiem

Till some roofed creek or tangle of green lawyer
Had gripped me . . .

We shared a cabin on the southbound ferry.
Perhaps he came too late. I do not know.

Christmas 1943

Mud-crabs were talkative on Sundays
Along the flats below the farm;
Swinging a pitchfork in the barn
I put on muscle and grew sideways.

Charlie, the bee-keeping brother,
Coddled his rheumatic heart

And spoke of Christ; the young one, Walter.
Taught me how to split dry logs with a mallet

And work the hillside plough.
Uneasy, celibate,
Dropping asleep I often heard
The grass in the orchard grow,

The rain throbbing in the creekbed,
And dreamt of a girl I bought
A ticket for on a tram in Castle Street,
Loaded with sorrow like an unhatched egg.

A Family Photograph 1939

Waves bluster up the bay and through the throat
Of the one-span bridge. My brother shoots
The gap alone
Like Charon sculling in his boat
Above the squids and flounders. With the jawbone
Of a sperm whale he fights the town,
Dances on Fridays to the cello
With black-haired sluts. My father in his gumboots
Is up a ladder plucking down
The mottled autumn-yellow
Dangling torpedo clusters
Of passion fruit for home-made wine.
My mother in the kitchen sunshine
Tightens her dressing gown,
Chops up carrots, onions, leeks,
For thick hot winter soup. No broom or duster
Will shift the English papers piled on chairs
And left for weeks.

I, in my fuggy room at the top of the stairs,
A thirteen-year-old schizophrene,
Write poems, wish to die,
And watch the long neat mason-fly
Malignantly serene
Arrive with spiders dopier than my mind
And build his clay dungeons inside the roller blind.

Concrete Grady at the Saturday Novena

Today the earth smokes like an iron dish
With the breath of trees and men. We go,
Lady, to your novena up the slow
Harbour steps. In the monastery church
The sea-sick candles blaze like little fish;
I falter in the porch
Because Leviathan, your Son, inside
Waits with tremendous jaws to swallow down
My sin, the squid-white follies of the town,
Turning to ambergris our human pride.

Mother, must I be Jonah? Yes; I hear
The song of those who sleep in the belly of God.
Your crowned face beckons me, a gilded nod
That smashes to my heart. Punch-drunk I come
While Satan whispers gruffly in my ear,
'Old stumblebum,
Hypocrite, think, think, you could be stuck
In a Chinese moll. *She* beckons you to death,
The treadmill, Father Hogan's fetid breath!'
– I see him fall, a plumed bird, lightning-struck.

The Tree

Nothing was evil then. The editing came later.
Thirty years back, down time's rock shaft, I see,
Too early for the heart-and-arrow sign,
A tree of vulvas oozing golden resin
Where I and my wire-muscled cousin
Climbed endlessly. Its bird-shit-spattered branches
Invoked the gross maternal mystery
That fed his life and mine.

Smoking my father's tobacco in a sly
Tree house, or edging up a shaking mast
To a cradle open to the sky,
Riding those giant fronded arms,
I seemed to be included by
The wind in its long conversation
About some secret known to birds or men;
Perhaps what made my uncle die;

Something too hard for words. My cousin,
Climbing the ladder after me,
Would call me barmy, slither down the tree
Like an opossum, wrestle with
Scissors and headlock, order me to try on
His boxing gloves. And fighting him
I quite forgot I carried in my pocket
Green macrocarpa nuts, the seeds of time.

The Boys

I cannot go
Where the boys go, up creek in wet canoes
In summer, past the cattle ground,

Till at the rock bend
Their flailing paddles bruise
A black wide looking-glass where ngaios gaze
And spread their thighs,
A hole going down to the world's centre,

Waiting to swallow the sun. I think I am
The invisible drowned man floating there
Above a mud couch, nuzzled
By eel and trout, too tightly held
By the weed's arms to rise
Again to the dazzle of day, the shouting boys,
The boats, the gorse-pods blown across the water.

At Serrières

Blue water of the Rhône in its rock bed
Stalling, circling in pools behind
The island lousy with snakes: down I sank
With stones inside my bathing dress
To the mud bottom, to walk like a crab,

All that green summer drank
Air, knowledge. Bitter tough-skinned grapes
In a wild hilltop vineyard,
And the days, the days, like long loaves
Broken in half, as I fished with a cord

And a pierced stone for Yvette, the manager's daughter
Killing hens in the hotel courtyard.
That castle where my brother broke his arm,
Yes: convolvulus vines, starved ghosts in dungeons . . .
But the family album does not include

The new guitar of sex I kept on twanging
Inside the iron virgin
Of the little smelly dyke, or that Easter Sunday,
Through a chink in the bedclothes, watching my mother dressing:
The heavy thighs, the black bush of hair.

Those wild red grapes were bitter
Though you could not tell them, by just looking, from the table kind.

The Hollow Place

On the waste low headland
Below the road, above the plunging sea,
I would climb often round the crumbling face
Where flax bushes precariously
Gave something to grip: then I'd stand
Alive in the hollow place
That meant . . . well, I must describe it: a bent cleft
In limestone rock above a pool
Of fluttering scum; bushes to the left,
And an overhang. The passage was dark and cool,
Three yards long perhaps, hidden from any eye
Not acquainted; and the air
Tainted by some odour as if the earth sweated
In primeval sleep. I did nothing there;
There was nothing to do but listen to some greater I
Whose language was silence. Again and again I came
And was healed of the daftness, the demon in the head
And the black knot in the thighs, by a silence that
Accepted all. Not knowing I would come again,
My coat of words worn very thin,
Knocking, as if lame,

With a dry stick on the dumb
Door of the ground, and crying out:
'Open, mother. Open. Let me in.'

The Cold Hub

Lying awake on a bench in the town belt,
Alone, eighteen, more or less alive,
Lying awake to the sound of clocks,
The railway clock, the Town Hall clock,
And the Varsity clock, genteel, exact
As a Presbyterian conscience,
I heard the hedgehogs chugging round my bench,
Colder than an ice-axe, colder than a bone,
Sweating the booze out, a spiritual Houdini
Inside the padlocked box of winter, time and craving.

Sometimes I rolled my coat and put it under my head.
And when my back got frozen, I put it on again.
I thought of my father and mother snoring at home
While the fire burnt out in feathery embers.
I thought of my friends each in their own house
Lying under blankets, tidy as dogs or mice.
I thought of my med. student girlfriend
Dreaming of horses, cantering brown-eyed horses,
In her unreachable bed, wrapped in a yellow quilt,

And something bust inside me, like a winter clod
Cracked open by the frost. A sense of being at
The absolute unmoving hub
From which, to which, the intricate roads went.
Like Hemingway, I call it *nada*:
Nada, the Spanish word for nothing.

Nada; the belly of the whale; nada;
Nada; the little hub of the great wheel;
Nada; the house on Cold Mountain
Where the east and the west wall bang together;
Nada; the drink inside the empty bottle.
You can't get there unless you are there.
The hole in my pants where the money falls out,
That's the beginning of knowledge; *nada*.

It didn't last for long; it never left me.
I knew that I was *nada*. Almost happy,
Stiff as a giraffe, I called in later
At an early grill, had coffee, chatted with the boss.

That night, drunk again, I slept much better
At the bus station, in a broom cupboard.

The Last Judgement

The children have more sense than to be sad
Tucked down – my daughter loiters and my son
Grizzles about a picture he'd begun
And screwed and burnt. Hugging can knock the bad
Mood back; long hugging. I'm left alone to look

At Breughel's *Judgement* in a book
Which proves by symbols the Unconscious Mind
Makes Hell and Heaven. Are you blind,
Old man? the smoke of Tartarus
Was never hard to find;

Quando judex est venturus . . .
My friend at half-past five in a lounge bar

Told me he thought the world had hair around it
Like Breughel's whale's-mouth Pit
Down which an army plunges. He'd just bought

The latest make of English car
With automatic gears for his third wife
To ride in, ride, self-taught,
Past the skull signs, to endless life,
To Mary Baker Eddy's world of thought

Or the stony gully of Jehoshaphat
Where the dead rise. I know that boneless mouth,
The owl, the dragon and the fish;
Long hugging cannot make it nice
To be laid out alive upon a dish

Under the eye and claw of the clever cat . . .
But there is pity, pity, wind of the South
That blows to some rose garden where
My dead grandmother in her old cane chair
Smiles at the Judge and strokes the quivering mice.

Martyrdom

Balancing on two boards up under
The spouting I fiddle with a brush.
My wife tells me I'm slow;
I just wonder
Will Our Lady grab me if I dive
Thirty feet
Down like a bull seal to the concrete?
I doubt it.

In the kitchen she sings, *'Ko tenei te po,'*
Like an Opunake thrush.
My rigours make her thrive;
I'm gaining merit.
My daughter grizzles down below
About some bad word someone said, or that
Fat plaster-eating mouse
Who camps under my bed.
She thinks I'm an acrobat
In a travelling show. This night. My son
Brings me a spider in a bottle – red
Like old burnt clay its hypodermic head –
Look, Daddy, look! The house
Of Atreus glitters in the midday sun.

The Buried Stream

Tonight our cat, Tahi, who lately lost
One eyebrow, yowls in the bush with another cat;

Our glass Tibetan ghost-trap has caught no ghost
Yet, but jangles suspended in the alcove that

We varnished and enlarged. Unwisely I have read
Sartre on Imagination – very dry, very French,

An old hound with noises in his head
Who dreams the hunt is on, yet fears the stench

Of action – he teaches us that human choice
Is rarely true or kind. My children are asleep.

Something clatters in the kitchen. I hear the voice
Of the buried stream that flows deep, deep,

Through caves I cannot enter, whose watery rope
Tugs my divining rod with the habit some call hope.

On Reading Yevtushenko

When the mine exploded at Kaitangata
Trucks flew out as if from the barrel of a gun,
Trucks and truckers, bodies of men,
Or so my father told me;
                              and far down
In those dark passages they heard faintly
The waves of the sea hammer
Above their heads.
                    My father's hands are corded
With swollen veins, but my hands are thinner
And my thoughts are cold, Zhenya Yevtushenko;
They are covered with black dust.
                                 Reading you
I remember our own strangled Revolution:
1935. The body of our Adam was dismembered
By statisticians.
                  I would like to meet you
Quietly in a café, where hoboes and freckled girls
Drink, talk; not to pump you; only to revalue in your company
Explosions, waves of the sea.

Waipatiki Beach

1

Under rough kingly walls the black-and-white
Sandpiper treads on stilts the edges

Of the lagoon, whose cry is like
A creaking door. We came across the ridges

By a bad road, banging in second gear,
Into the only world I love:

This wilderness. Through the noon light rambling clear
Foals and heifers in the green paddocks move.

The sun is a shepherd. Once I would have wanted
The touch of flesh to cap and seal my joy,

Not yet having sorted it out. Bare earth, bare sea,
Without fingers crack open the hard ribs of the dead.

2

If anyone, I'd say the oldest Venus
Too early for the books, ubiquitous,

The manifold mother to whom my poems go
Like ladders down – at the mouth of the gully

She had left a lip of sand for the coarse grass to grow.
Also the very quiet native bee

Loading his pollen bags. We parked the car
There, and walked on

Down to the bank of the creek, where the water ran under
A froth of floating sticks and pumice stone,

And saw in the dune's clasp the burnt black
Trunk of a totara the sea had rolled back.

3

Her lion face, the skull-brown Hekate
Ruling my blood since I was born,

I had not found it yet. I and my son
Went past the hundred-headed cabbage tree

At the end of the beach, barefooted, in danger of
Stones falling from the overhang, and came

On a bay too small to have a name
Where flax grew wild on the shoulder of the bluff

And a waterfall was weeping. A sheep leapt and stood
Bleating at us beyond a tangle of driftwood

And broken planks. Behind us floated in the broad noon
Sky that female ghost, the daylight moon.

4

A leper's anger in the moon's disc, or
The long-tongued breaker choked by sand,

Spell out my years like Pharaoh's wheat and husk –
I walk and look for shelter from the wind

Where many feet have trodden
Till silence rises and the beach is hidden.

An Ode to the Reigning Monarch on the Occasion of Her Majesty's Visit to Pig Island

Madam, I beg to quarrel with
Your trip across the water –
Pig Island needs no English myth
To keep its guts in order,
Though our half-witted housewives yearn
At your image on the TV screen.

Forgive me that I cannot praise
The Civil Service State
Whose blueprints falsify the maze
It labours to create,
And plants above that sticky mess
Yourself in an icing sugar dress.

The dead who drink at Bellamys
Are glad when school kids clap
A Fairy Queen who justifies
The nabob and the bureaucrat,
In a land where a wharfie's daughter can
Marry some day the squatter's son.

While the stuffed monkey, dog and sow,
Play ludo in the void,
The Auckland pavements carry now
Six hundred unemployed,
And the bought clerks who sneer at them
Will crowd to kiss your diadem.

The girls in Arohata jail
Are very rarely dressed in silk –
Let us take a Glasgow cocktail

Bubbling coal gas into milk,
Drink up to Mary, Kate and Lou,
No better and no worse than you.

Before my birth your soldiers made
A football of my skull
At Mud Farm when they crucified
My father on a pole
Because he would not take a gun
And kill another working man.

I give you now to end our talk
A toast you will not like:
McSwiney the Lord Mayor of Cork
Who died on hunger strike.
It took him eighty days to drown
In the blood and shit that floats the Crown.

While Big Ben bangs out stroke on stroke
And the circus wheel spins round,
The Maori looks at Holyoake
And Holyoake looks at the ground,
And there will be more things to say
When the Royal yacht has sailed away.

Shingle Beach Poem

There is (conveniently) a hollow space
Between the upper and the lower jaws

Of the world serpent. There, as if all days
Were one, the children whack

Their seaweed balls, brag, tussle, comb the shores
For little crabs. There's no road back

To the dream time, and I endure instead
This hunger to be nothing. I supplicate

Dark heaven for the peace of that woman they
Lifted out of the breakers yesterday,

With blue deaf ears, whom Poseidon banged on the kelp-beds
Though she was a good swimmer, her body oatmeal-white

Spotted with shingle. To and fro
She was rolled by the undertow.

This I understand. Sister, remember
Us who wrestle yet in the coil of life's hunger.

The Farm

Calves with blue cloudy eyes
Thrust their heads into the pail

And snorted bubbles. I remember the rise
Where Walter and I split old, dry logs with the maul

Below the railway line. The whole farm
Is hidden somewhere in my guts, as if

I'd swallowed it: the creek, the byres, the haybarn,
The crumbs of wood and resin in the sawpit.

All tracks led outward then. I did not see
How bones and apples rot under the tree

In cocksfoot grass, or guess the size
Of the world, a manuka nut in the sun's gaze.

Then

Like gin in a clear glass the currents flowed
Beyond the low scrub hills, and we were made
Free of the springs of the underworld

(Light from the day's end, the year's death, rising
In darkening heaven): we danced
There, if I remember rightly,

To the tune of a concertina somebody played
In the little bar room. A man dancing with a man.
You could never talk when you were drunk;

I, stumble-footed, now as then.

East Coast Journey

About twilight we came to the whitewashed pub
On a knuckle of land above the bay

Where a log was riding and the slow
Bird-winged breakers cast up spray.

One of the drinkers round packing cases had
The worn face of a kumara god,

Or so it struck me. Later on
Lying awake in the veranda bedroom

In great dryness of mind I heard the voice of the sea
Reverberating, and thought: As a man

Grows older he does not want beer, bread, or the prancing flesh,
But the arms of the eater of life, Hine-nui-te-po,

With teeth of obsidian and hair like kelp
Flashing and glimmering at the edge of the horizon.

The Watch

That bad year when we were both apart
The statues in the churches were covered in purple
And north of Auckland I woke to see a sail-shaped rock
Standing up from the endless water. The boat
Lumbered. The stink of vomit and vodka stuck
To the craters in my brain. It isn't simple
To be oneself. The void inside
Grows troublesome. At midday a yellow bee
Flew over the hummocked waves as if he were searching
For clover in a paddock. At night the boat stopped lurching
And I came on deck for the graveyard watch.
Sea, air, night;
The numbers had been rubbed from the clock.
At the deck's edge a sailor in dungarees
Let down a hook and a line.
Inside my head I heard the voice of another man:

'In Circe's palace I fell drunk
Missing the steep ladder;

I came before you to this den.
Plant above my bones that oar
I used to tug, strong at the rower's bench.
When your throats are dry and the keg is empty
Remember me . . .'

New Zealand
(for Monte Holcroft)

These unshaped islands, on the sawyer's bench,
Wait for the chisel of the mind,
Green canyons to the south, immense and passive,
Penetrated rarely, seeded only
By the deer-culler's shot, or else in the north
Tribes of the shark and the octopus,
Mangroves, black hair on a boxer's hand.

The founding fathers with their guns and bibles.
Botanist, whaler, added bones and names
To the land, to us a bridle
As if the id were a horse: the swampy towns
Like dreamers that struggle to wake,

Longing for the poet's truth
And the lover's pride. Something new and old
Explores its own pain, hearing
The rain's choir on curtains of grey moss
Or fingers of the Tasman pressing
On breasts of hardening sand, as actors
Find their own solitude in mirrors,

As one who has buried his dead,
Able at last to give with an open hand.

[104]

Pig Island Letters
(to Maurice Shadbolt)

1

The gap you speak of – yes, I find it so,
The menopause of the mind. I think of it
As a little death, practising for the greater,
For the undertaker who won't have read
Your stories or my verse –
Or that a self had died
Who handled ideas like bombs,

In that bare southern town
At a party on a cold night
Men seen as ghosts, women like trees walking,
Seen from the floor, a forest of legs and bums
For the climbing boy, the book-bred one.

And this, the moment of art, can never stay.
Wives in the kitchen cease to smile as we go
Into the gap itself, the solid night
Where poor drunks fear the icy firmament:
Man is a walking grave,

That is where I start from. Though often
Where the Leith Stream wandered down
Its culvert, crinkled labia of blossom
On the trees beside the weir
Captured and held the fugitive
From time, from self, from the iron pyramid,

These were diversions. Give my love
To Vic. He is aware of
The albatross. In the Otago storms

Carrying spray to salt the landward farms
The wind is a drunkard. Whoever can listen
Long enough will write again.

2

From an old house shaded with macrocarpas
Rises my malady.
Love is not valued much in Pig Island
Though we admire its walking parody,

That brisk gaunt woman in the kitchen
Feeding the coal range, sullen
To all strangers, lest one should be
Her antique horn-red Satan.

Her man, much baffled, grousing in the pub,
Discusses sales
Of yearling lambs, the timber in a tree
Thrown down by autumn gales,

Her daughter, reading in her room
A catalogue of dresses,
Can drive a tractor, goes to Training College,
Will vote on the side of the Bosses,

Her son is moodier, has seen
An angel with a sword
Standing above the clump of old man manuka
Just waiting for the word

To overturn the cities and the rivers
And split the house like a rotten totara log.

Quite unconcerned he sets his traps for 'possums
And whistles to his dog.

The man who talks to the masters of Pig Island
About the love they dread
Plaits ropes of sand, yet I was born among them
And will lie some day with their dead.

3

That other Baxter the Sectarian
Said that the bodies of the damned will burn
Like stubble thrown into a red-hot oven
On Judgement Day. In Calvin's town
At seventeen I thought I might see
Not fire but water rise

From the shelves of surf beyond St Clair
To clang the dry bell. Gripping
A pillow wife in bed
I did my convict drill,
And when I made a mother of the keg
The town split open like an owl's egg
Breaking the ladders down. It was
Perhaps the winter of beginning:

Frost standing up like stubble in the streets
Below the knees of Maori Hill,
Looking for the last simplicity
And nothing to explain it in the books,
In a room where the wind clattered the blind-cord
In the bed of a girl with long plaits
I found the point of entry,
The place where father Adam died.

[107]

Meanwhile a boy with dog and ferret
Climbed up the gorse track from the sea
To the turn at the top of the gully
Twelve paces past the cabbage tree,
And saw from the crest of the hill
Pillars of rain move on the dark sea,
A cloud of fire rise up above Japan,
God's body blazing on damnation's tree.

Thank you for the letter. I read your book
Five days ago: it has the slow
Imperceptible wingbeat of the hawk
Above the dry scrublands. The kill is there
In the Maori riverbed below
Where bones glitter. I could tell
Of other matters, but not now.

4

The censor will not let my lines reveal
Pig Island spinning on the potter's wheel.

A skinny wench in jeans with a kea's eye:
The rack on which our modern martyrs die.

I prophesy these young delinquent bags
Will graduate to grim demanding hags.

Our women chiefly carry in their bones
The curse that stuck to the scattered oven stones.

How often Remuera girls abort
Has not been mentioned in the Hunn Report.

Holyoake yammering from a kauri stump –
God save us all! I need a stomach pump.

Sea-eggs, puha, pork, and kumara:
The Maori owned the land. I have a camera.

Though Freud and God may bless the marriage vow
You must know how to work the hillside plough.

The sun is warm, the nosebag smells of hay,
The wind is blowing from the north today.

You who were pulled apart by four draught horses,
Saint Hippolytus, pray for us!

5

Long ago, in a ghostly summer,
Somebody held a burning-glass
Above the ants on mountains of crumbed asphalt
So that one lived, another died:
The hawk's eye, the man in the sky
With his vats of poison cloud
Like Jeyes Fluid. Above the old river
The bridge was a broad mother,
And the small drum of the heart beat loud,

Where the salt gush flowed in
Hooking the fish of Maui on a pin.

To learn the tricks of water
From the boathouse keeper's daughter
Is the task of time. I make

My genuflection at an iron altar
Before the black fish rise, the weather break.

6

The hope of the body was coherent love
As if the water sighing on the shores
Would penetrate the hardening muscle, loosen
Whatever had condemned itself in us:
Not the brown flagon, not the lips
Anonymously pressed in the dim light,
But a belief in bodily truth rising
From fountains of Bohemia and the night,

The truth behind the lie behind the truth
That Fairburn told us, gaunt
As the great moa, throwing the twisted blunt
Darts in a pub this side of Puhoi – 'No
Words make up for what we had in youth.'
For what we did not have: that hunger caught
Each of us, and left us burnt,
Split open, grit-dry, sifting the ash of thought.

7

This love that heals like a crooked limb
In each of us, source of our grief,
Could tell us if we cared to listen, why
Sons by mayhem, daughters by harlotry
Pluck down the sky's rage on settled houses:
The thin girl and the cornerboy
Whose angers mask their love

Unwind, unwind the bandages
That hide in each the hope of joy.

For me it is the weirs that mention
The love that we destroy
By long evasion, politics and art,
And speech that is a kind of contraception:
A streetlight flashing down
On muscled water, bodies in the shade,
Tears on a moonwhite face, the voice
Of time from the grave of water speaking to
Those who are lucky to be sad.

8

When I was only semen in a gland
Or less than that, my father hung
From a torture post at Mud Farm
Because he would not kill. The guards
Fried sausages, and as the snow came darkly
I feared a death by cold in the cold groin
And plotted revolution. His black and swollen thumbs
Explained the brotherhood of man,

But he is old now in his apple garden
And we have seen our strong Antaeus die
In the glass castle of the bureaucracies
Robbing our bread of salt. Shall Marx and Christ
Share beds this side of Jordan? I set now
Unwillingly these words down:

Political action in its source is pure,
Human, direct, but in its civil function
Becomes the jail it laboured to destroy.

[111]

9

Look at the simple caption of success,
The poet as family man,
Head between thumbs at mass, nailing a trolley
Letting the tomcat in:
Then turn the hourglass over, find the other
Convict self, incorrigible, scarred
With what the bottle and the sex games taught.
The black triangle, the whips of sin.
The first gets all his meat from the skull-faced twin,
Sharpening a dagger out of a spoon,
Struggling to speak through the gags of a poem:
When both can make a third my work is done.

Nor will the obituary ever indicate
How much we needed friends,
Like Fitz at the National
Speaking of his hydatid cyst,
A football underneath the lung,
Or Lowry in Auckland: all who held the door
And gave us space for art,
Time for the re-shaping of the heart:
Those whom the arrow-makers honour least,
Companions to the manbeast,
One man in many, touching the flayed hide gently,
A brother to the artist and a nurse.

The trees rustle as October comes
And fantails batter on the glass,
Season when the day nurse tuts and hums
Laying out pills and orange juice
For one who walks the bridge of dread
As oedema sets in,

While through the bogs and gullies of Pig Island
Bellies are beaten like skin drums
In pup tents, under flax or lupin shade,

As if the sun were a keg. And this man
On the postman's round will meditate
The horn of Jacob withered at the root
Or quirks of weather. None
Grow old easily. The poem is
A plank laid over the lion's den.

10

To outflank age – a corrugated shack
With fried pauas in the pan,
Beside a bay somewhere, grandchildren in tribes
Wrestling in the long grass, seawater, sleep,
While cloud and green tree like sisters keep
The last door for the natural man.

It will be what it is, half-life,
For the mystery requires
A victim – Marsyas the manbeast
Hung up and flayed on a fir tree,
Or a death by inches, catheter and wife
Troubling an old man's vanity.

11

Tonight I read my son a story
About the bees of Baiame, who tell the east wind
To blow down rain, so that the flowers grow

In dry Australia, and the crow wirinun
Who jailed the west wind in a hollow log:

My son who is able to build a tree house
With vine ladders, my son
In his brown knitted jersey and dungarees,
Makes clowns and animals, a world of creatures
To populate paradise,

And when he hands me easily
The key of entry, my joy must be dissembled
Under a shutter of horn, a dark lantern,
In case it should too brightly burn,

Because the journey has begun
Into the land where the sun is silent
And no one may enter the tree house
That hides the bones of a child in the forest of a man.

12

The dark wood Dante wrote of
Is no more than the self, the wandering gulf
That calls itself a man, seen
Through the dark prism of self-love:
Under the leafy screen
Lion, leopard, wolf,
Show by their anger we are not yet slain.

Our loves have tied us to the wheel
From which it is death to be unbound,
Yet unexpected, unpredictable,
Like speckled rain that falls on a wave,

Come the light fingers on the wound,
Or where the marae meets the cattle hill
The face of Beatrice moving in the grove.

13

Stat crux dum volvitur orbis: I will sing
In the whale's belly.
                    'Great Mother of God
Sweeten my foul breath. I wait for a death.
Cradle me, Lady, on the day they carry
My body down the bush track to the road
To the rollers of the decorous van.
The leper's stump, the thick voice of the drunk.
Are knocking at Nazareth. I am a naked man.'

'How can I let you in?
The time for talk has gone;
A mountain is the threshold stone.'

'Mother, I come alone.
No books, no bread
Are left in my swag.'

'Why are your hands not clean?'

'There was no soap in the whole damned town.'

'God's grace has need of man's apology.'

'Your face is my theology.'

'Yes; but I gave you a jewel to bring.'

[115]

'In the thick gorse of the gully
I lost your signet ring.'

'Why should I listen then?'

'On Skull Hill there was none,
No scapular, no sign,
Only the words, *I thirst*,
When the blood of a convict burst
From the body of your son.'

'You may come in.'

Is it like that? At least I know no better;
After a night of argument
Mythical, theological, political,
Somebody has the sense to get a boat
And row out towards the crayfish rocks
Where, diving deep, the downward swimmer
Finds fresh water rising up,
A mounded water breast, a fountain,
An invisible tree whose roots cannot be found;

As that wild nymph of water rises
So does the God in man.

Letter to Robert Burns

King Robert, on your anvil stone
Above the lumbering Octagon,
To you I raise a brother's horn
Led by the wandering unicorn
Of total insecurity.

[116]

Never let your dead eye look
Up from Highland Mary's book
To the fat scrag-end of the Varsity.
Kilmarnock hag and dominie
Watch there the grey Leith water drum
With laughter from a bird's beak
At what their learning has left out.
They tried to make my devil speak
With the iron boot of education
(Psychology, French, Latin) –
But though they drove the wedges in
Till the blood and marrow spouted out,
That spirit was dumb.

Robert, only a heart I bring,
No gold of words to grace a king,
Nor can a stranger lift that flail
That cracked the wall of Calvin's jail
And earned you the lead garland of
A people's moralising love,
Till any Scotsman with the shakes
Can pile on your head his mistakes
And petrify a boozaroo
Reciting *Tam o' Shanter* through;
And there's an old black frost that freezes
Apollo's balls and the blood of Jesus
In this dry, narrow-gutted town.
Often enough I stumbled down
From Maori Hill to the railway station
(When Aussie gin was half the price)
Making my Easter meditation
In the wilderness of fire and ice
Where a Puritan gets his orientation.

King Robert with the horn of stone!
Perhaps your handcuffs were my own;
Your coffin-cradle was the blank
Medusa conscience of a drunk
That hankers for the purity
Of an imagined infancy,
And after riding seven whores
Approaches God upon all fours,
Crying, 'O thou great Incubus,
Help me or turn me to a walrus!'
And in hangover weeps to see
A playing child or a walnut tree.
If, lying in the pub latrine,
You muttered, 'Take me back to Jean,'
The reason for your mandrake groans
Is wrapped like wire around my bones.

Not too far from the Leith water
My mother saw the mandrake grow
And pulled it. A professor's daughter,
She told me some time after how
She had been frightened by a cow
So that the birth-sac broke too soon
And on the twenty-ninth of June
Prematurely I looked at the walls
And yelled. The Plunket nurse ran in
To scissor off my valued foreskin,
But one thing staggered that grimalkin:
Poets are born with three balls.

Biology, mythology,
Go underground when the bookmen preach,
And I must thank the lass who taught me
My catechism at Tunnel Beach;

For when the hogmagandie ended
And I lay thunder-struck and winded,
The snake-haired Muse came out of the sky
And showed her double axe to me.
Since then I die and do not die.
'Jimmy,' she said, 'you are my ugliest son;
I'll break you like a herring-bone.'

I fill my pipe with black tobacco
And watch a dead man's ember glow.

Seven Year Old Poet
(after Rimbaud)

The mother, shutting the schoolbook, walked off blind
And well content, not seeing the hatred of work behind
The child's bumpy forehead, and under the blue eyes
An enemy self not built to fraternise.

Obedient he'd drudge all day; a quite
Intelligent boy; but somehow the sour bite
Of hypocrisy showed in his habits. Passing along
Mildewed passages, he'd stick out his tongue
And clench both fists in his groin, watching the spark
Of tiny specks that floated in the dark
Under his eyelids.
                 If a door on the evening air
Was open, you'd see him gasp, half up the stair,
Like a drying frog, under the gulf of day
That hung from the roofs. He'd hide himself away
In summer, clubbed flat, torpid, in the dell
Of a latrine, peacefully drinking the smell,

And it was cool there.
                              Sometimes when winter moonlight
Had washed the bushes, and antiseptic night
Drove out the daytime odours, he'd lie at the foot
Of a wall behind the house, like a cabbage root
Half underground, rubbing his eyes in order
To see visions, and hear each scabbed leaf shudder.
Quite tragic! His companions were those bent
Children whose clothes have a smell of excrement,
Old-fashioned, black-earth-knuckled, sometimes toothless,
Talking together in idiot gentleness.

And if, catching him out in some foul act
Of pity, his worrying Mother grubbed round the fact
For evidence, out of sick love he'd raise
A screen, and she'd believe it – that blue-eyed liar's gaze!

The seven-year-old would make up yarns inside
His own head, of the wastes where Freedom glows like a bride:
Savannahs, great trees, suns and shores – He'd rush
To coloured magazines, and stare and blush
At Spanish and Italian girls.
                                        From time to time a wild
Tomboy, the next-door family's dragged-up child
Brown-eyed and skittish, would jump on his back from behind –
Just eight years old – tossing her plaits; and blind
As a weasel in a burrow, he'd use his teeth
To bite her bare arse from underneath
She never wore pants) – then, bruised by her heels and her claws,
He'd mooch to his room with the taste of her flesh in his jaws.

Sundays in winter, hair flattened with brilliantine,
At the pedestal table, reading a salad-green-
Edged-Bible – he hated it. In the alcove at night

Millstone dreams would grind him, till day's light
Drying the sweats of terror, pink as a dove,
Came back to the gable.
                              God he did not love,
But men, men he saw at sunset, dark
From the sun's glare, strolling in smocks to the park
Where the town criers would make the crowd come
To grizzle or laugh at their words, by the thrice-heard roll of a drum.
– He dreamt of the grassy field, where light in waves
Rose up, with a smell like bread, from the groined caves
Waist-high, a place for love!
                              And more than all else
He liked what is dark: as when, shut from the bells
In the barn of his room – not minding the icy damp
Of the blue walls, he would read of a rebel camp
Among drowned forests, leaden skies, great flowers
Of flesh in starry woods, Andean towers,
Giddiness, flight – while the street chattered below –
Face down, his blue eyes flickering to and fro.
He would live the novel – alone, stretched out on the pale
Coarse linen that caught the wind, a ship in full sail.

Tomcat

This tomcat cuts across the
zones of the respectable
through fences, walls, following
other routes, his own. I see
the sad whiskered skull-mouth fall
wide, complainingly, asking

to be picked up and fed, when
I thump up the steps through bush

at 4 p.m. He has no
dignity, thank God! has grown
older, scruffier, the ash-
black coat sporting one or two

flowers like round stars, badges
of bouts and fights. The snake head
is seamed on top with rough scars:
old Samurai! He lodges
in cellars, and the tight furred
scrotum drives him into wars

as if mad. Yet tumbling on
the rug looks female, Turkish-
trousered. His bagpipe shriek at
sluggish dawn dragged me out in
pyjamas to comb the bush
(he being under the vet

for septic bites): the old fool
stood, body hard as a board,
heart thudding, hair on end, at
the house corner, terrible,
yelling at something. They said,
'Get him doctored.' I think not.

At Days Bay

To lie on a beach after
looking at old poems: how
slow untroubled by any
grouch of mine or yours, Father
Ocean tumbles in the bay
alike with solitary

divers, cripples, yelling girls
and pipestem kids. He does what
suits us all; and somewhere – there,
out there, where the high tight sails
are going – he wears a white
death flag of foam for us, far

out, for when we want it. So
on Gea's breast, the broad nurse
who bears with me, I think of
adolescence: that sad boy
I was, thoughts crusted with ice
on the treadmill of self-love,

Narcissus damned, who yet brought
like a coal in a hollow
stalk, the seed of fire that runs
through my veins now. I praise that
sad boy now, who having no
hope, did not blow out his brains.

The Ballad of Grady's Dream

One clink black night in June
Concrete Grady sat
Between the knees of the pines
With Old Jack Flynn his mate,

And through the harbour fog
The guts of Wellington
Glowed like a great morgue
Where even the cops had gone.

'I had a dream,' said Grady –
Flynn said, 'Stuff your dream!
I'd give my ballocks now
For a bucket of steam.'

'I had a dream,' said Grady,
When I slept in Mulligan's woodyard
Under a wad of roofing iron;
I was a white bird,

'And then a gale caught me
And threw me north;
There was nothing left standing
On the bare-arsed earth,

'And I thought of the time in Crete
When we jammed the Bren gun
And the paratroops came over
Like washing on a line,

'And you'll remember, Jack,
Because you were there,
We shot twelve prisoners
In Imvros village square;

'Because the wind blew me
To the door of a stone barn,
And the Nazi lads were sitting
At a table playing cards –

'*Sergeant, come in,* they said,
We've kept you a place –
And when they turned I saw
The red-hot bone in each one's face,

'So I let the wind carry
Me out past Kapiti
In the belly of the storm above
A thousand miles of sea,

'Till I came to a blind cliff
That got no sun,
Deep as the cunning of Hell
And high as the trouble of man.

'There was one gap in it
Where only a bird could fly;
I said the Hail Mary
And threaded the needle's eye,

'And there in a green garden
I saw the Tramways Band
And a crowd of people walking
With flagons in their hands,

'And on a bullock wagon
The Host Itself with seven nuns,
And one of them had the face
Of Rose O'Rourke when she was young.'

'You've struck it there,' said Flynn,
'She'd be a bit of all right;
But I'd give old Rose the go-by
For a bottle of steam tonight.'

High Wind at Hokio

That day the gale blew hard, if
I remember rightly – so
we left the car by the bridge
and trod the rough grooved beach, deaf
with the air's army that blew
snakes of sand from the dune's edge

to fill our shoes. A low plain
of toetoe opened her knees
on the tumbling brown-white flood
of waves like the chaos when
Earth was born . . . But what bound us
together and apart did

not slacken – mother, father,
daughter, son – held by the yoke
that rubs us raw yet teaches
a kind of truth: that nowhere
can the heart finally speak
or cease burning, as air touches

the dry sand and makes it flow,
or as that Maori girl rode out
on a sideways cantering
horse, from the bridge where a boy
chucked hollow reeds on the mute
creek, against the gale blowing.

Postman

To set a bound to chaos
(put it that way) the streets are
named, the houses numbered – but
foot-slogging over wet grass
or asphalt, the postman's dour
thought will sprout new chaos, not

original – so I find
as the housewives' donkey, bare-
shirted in the rain. The small
dogs muttering from the ground
smell me out, as I stagger,
and nip at the lifted heel

from paranoid love. I plod
up Motueka, Colway,
Karamu, each cold street a
dragon, and I stuck inside
the arse-pipe, a mildewed, slow-
ly moving turd. These roads were

built for the helicopter
or bullock-dray. The boxes
(made roomy, narrow, or with
iron flaps) exhibit your
private shapes, you grim ladies
married to a bourgeois death

who wait for letters from God,
and as my hand goes in, I
think kindly of you all – 'Yes,
Mrs Cokestacker, your strayed
parcel from Melbourne may be
in the bag' – or, the Abyss . . .

[127]

Thoughts of a Remuera Housewife

The tranquillisers on my
glass-topped table, black-and-green
pomegranate seeds, belong to
Pluto, that rough king – so I
have eaten six, to go in
quietly, quietly through

the dark mirror to his world
of chaos and the grave – 'Ann,
how strong you are!' my mother
said yesterday when the wild
pony all but threw Robin
under its hooves; I got her

to mount again. They don't know
I am Pluto's Queen . . . Oh yes,
I kept your letter saying
it was no good – what did you
mean by that? The drugged clouds race
over the gun-pit facing

all storm, where you stopped the car
and undid my jersey – now
my husband is undressing
and jerking at his collar
with the Bugs Bunny grin I
hated so . . . Our sort of dying

kept me young – my love, how high
the cocksfoot was! our own bed
walled in by soldier stalks of
grass – no one else could touch me,

among the lions' dens – mad,
happy, lost! In Pluto's cave

from granite thrones we watch the
ghosts whirling like snaking fog
quietly, quietly down
to their own urn, not to see
ever the sun's sweat-streaked flag
thunder again . . . In London

do they play Schubert or Brahms
in asbestos rooms? Do girls
bite your throat? When you turned me
into a violin (dreams
are what I go by) that pulse
in your neck . . . My Satan, why

did you not stay where flames rise
always up? You said no one
can fight the world . . . No; it's not
a world at all, but Pluto's
iron-black star, the quiet
planet furthest from the sun.

Great-Uncles and Great-Aunts

From Black Head to the bar of
Taieri Mouth, my father's
uncle scattered lupin seed
whose branches now give cover
to townbred couples who ride
out in cars, on bikes, and leave

pale condoms like balloons, or
shit among the fibred roots
that turn the dunes to soil – what
loose bright female bloom then fights
out of the bush's storm-wet
tabernacle! The colour

of blood or meditation
delicately hung, and the
pollen blown over the wide
stretch-marked belly of the sea –
Did strong chains in heart and head
choke back the airy dragon

that feeds on sighs, in those Job-
bearded crofters who split logs
for bluegum fences, and built
sod huts where now the gale brags?
Their bannock-meal lacking salt
grew mouldy – their wives could scrub

all stains from moleskin breeches
except Adam's dirt – and so
the lack ate inwardly like
fire in piled-up couchgrass too
green for it, billowing smoke –
a servant-girl's bruised haunches

up-ended in the barn, heads
split bloody at the caber-
tossing show – loud pipes, whisky . . .
O Mary, fetch a sugar
bag of snow to freshen my
great-aunts in their burning shrouds!

To a Print of Queen Victoria

I advise rest; the farmhouse
we dug you up in has been
modernised, and the people
who hung you as their ikon
against the long passage wall
are underground – Incubus

and excellent woman, we
inherit the bone acre
of your cages and laws. This
dull green land suckled at your
blood's *frigor Anglicanus,*
crowning with a housewife's tally

the void of Empire, does not
remember you – and certain
bloody bandaged ghosts rising
from holes of Armageddon
at Gallipoli or Sling
Camp, would like to fire a shot

through the gilt frame. I advise
rest, Madam; and yet the tomb
holds much that we must travel
barely without. Your print – 'from
an original pencil
drawing by the Marchioness

'of Granby, March, eighteen nine-
ty seven . . .' Little mouth, strong
nose and hooded eye – they speak
of half-truths my type have slung

out of the window, and lack
and feel the lack too late. Queen,

you stand most for the time of
early light, clay roads, great trees
unfelled, and the smoke from huts
where girls in sack dresses
stole butter . . . The small rain spits
today. You smile in your grave.

A Bucket of Blood for a Dollar
*(a conversation between Uncle Sam
and the Rt. Hon. Keith Holyoake,
Prime Minister of New Zealand)*

'You'll have to learn,' said Uncle Sam,
'The Yankee way of work
Now that you've joined in our crusade
Against the modern Turk;
The capital of the Commonwealth is
Not London, but New York.'

'Don't tell them that,' cried Holyoake,
'In Thames or Dannevirke.'

'Then use your loaf,' said Uncle Sam,
'Newspapers hit the eye;
If you get trouble from the men
That you can't bluff or buy,
Just spread the word that they're all Reds
And let the rumours fly.'

'I'll bang the drum,' said Holyoake –
And yet he heaved a sigh.

'Tell them straight,' said Uncle Sam,
'That it's a dirty war;
Mention the Freedom of the West
That we are fighting for;
But keep the money side of it
Well tucked behind the door.'

'I'll make it sound,' said Holyoake,
'Just like a football score.'

'Between the fights,' said Uncle Sam,
'They'll need some exercise;
There's a thousand brothels in Saigon
Where they can fraternise.
The peasants send their daughters there
When they have no rice.'

'Let's not be coarse,' said Holyoake,
Turning up his eyes.

'I fried a village,' said Uncle Sam,
'With the new phosphorus bomb
The day a Yankee Army nurse
Was killed by the Viet Cong;
A white dame's worth a million gooks –
In Asia, *we* belong.'

'Your chivalry,' said Holyoake,
'Puts angels in the wrong.'

'The newest way,' said Uncle Sam,
'To interrogate the brutes
Is a wet wire on the private parts
That half-electrocutes –
Though I do hate having to wash
Their vomit from my boots.'

[133]

'Don't talk so loud!' groaned Holyoake –
'We'll want the churches' votes.'

'I'm a simple chap,' sighed Holyoake,
'Politics hurt my head;
But why do you scrap with China
To the tune of a million dead
And sign a Pact with Russia,
When both of them are Red?'

'Get with it, Keith,' said Uncle Sam,
'We need the East for trade.'

'I'm a simple chap,' said Holyoake,
'Politics frighten me;
But whether it's frozen meat or men
We send across the sea,
We want good prices for our veal –
What can you guarantee?'

'Just name your price,' said Uncle Sam,
'And leave the rest to me.'

The Gunner's Lament
(for my wife, Te Kare)

A Maori gunner lay dying
In a paddyfield north of Saigon,
And he said to his pakeha cobber,
'I reckon I've had it, man!

'And if I could fly like a bird
To my old granny's whare

[134]

A truck and a winch would never drag
Me back to the Army.

'A coat and a cap and a well-paid job
Looked better than shovelling metal,
And they told me that Te Rauparaha
Would have fought in the Vietnam battle.

'On my last leave the town swung round
Like a bucket full of eels.
The girls liked the uniform
And I liked the girls.

'Like a bullock to the abattoirs
In the name of liberty
They flew me with a hangover
Across the Tasman Sea,

'And what I found in Vietnam
Was mud and blood and fire,
With the Yanks and the Reds taking turns
At murdering the poor,

'And I saw the reason for it
In a Viet Cong's blazing eyes –
We fought for the crops of kumara
And they are fighting for rice.

'So go and tell my sweetheart
To get another boy
Who'll cuddle her and marry her
And laugh when the bugles blow,

'And tell my youngest brother
He can have my shotgun

To fire at the ducks on the big lagoon,
But not to aim it at a man,

'And tell my granny to wear black
And carry a willow leaf,
Because the kid she kept from the cold
Has eaten a dead man's loaf,

'And go and tell Keith Holyoake
Sitting in Wellington,
However long he scrubs his hands
He'll never get them clean.'

The Strike

I saw the bright bones of Lenin
Glitter in the air above
The house we wintered in, ten or twelve
People like lovers, and the rising sun

On the harbour waves; Lenin's bright bones
In the air assembled, instructed
Us – 'Sharpen your axes
Against the tree of the State. I am necessity

Alive in the liberal grave' – We won the strike.
And fell back to our squabbles,
Counting shillings, drugs, cosmetics.

Lenin did not come back
To us. He slept again
In man's heart, the holy mountain.

The Lion Skin

The old man with a yellow flower on his coat
Came to my office, climbing twenty-eight steps,
With a strong smell of death about his person
From the caves of the underworld.
The receptionist was troubled by his breath
Understandably.
                    Not every morning tea break
Does Baron Saturday visit his parishioners
Walking stiffly, strutting almost,
With a cigar in his teeth – she might have remembered
Lying awake as if nailed by a spear
Two nights ago, with the void of her life
Glassed in a dark window – but suitably enough
She preferred to forget it.
                    I welcomed him
And poured him a glass of cherry brandy,
Talked with him for half an hour or so,
Having need of his strength, the skin of a dead lion,
In the town whose ladders are made of coffin wood.

The flower on his coat blazed like a dark sun.

On Possessing the Burns Fellowship 1966
(to Nicholas Zissermann)

Trees move slowly. The rain drops arrows
As on the Spartans from the Persian bowstring
Some while ago, across the tennis court
Behind the convent they hope to pull down,

And I who wrote in '62,
Dear ghosts, let me abandon
What cannot be held against
Hangmen and educators, the city of youth! –

Drink fresh percolated coffee, lounging
In the new house, at the flash red kitchen table,
A Varsity person, with an office
Just round the corner – what nonsense!

If there is any culture here
It comes from the black south wind
Howling above the factories
A handsbreadth from Antarctica,

Whatever the architect and planner
Least understand – not impossibly the voice
Of an oracle rising from that
Old battered green veranda

Beyond the board fence: a blood transfusion
From the earth's thick veins! As if
Caesar had died, and clouds, leaves, conspired to make
A dark mocking funeral wreath.

The Kraken

Where the sighing combs of water
Talk under broken jetties, and the long

Green flats of weed that Heaphy painted
Wait for the withheld kiss of the tide,

You who stroll on cliff-top boulders and
The abandoned gun-pit, do not

Expect the sea to break its own laws,
Or any Venus to be born

Out of the gulf's throat. Even the dead
Who made from this dug earth, proud air,

Something cruder than they meant,
Hang on museum walls. As night comes

You will hear from the lighthouse the foghorn speak
With a shuddering note, and watch how the kraken's wide

Blinding tendrils move like smoke
Over the rock neck, the muttering flats, the houses.

Dunedin Habits

A sense that no desire is ever answered
Except by death, if one should wish to be
Drunk night and day (having the money, the money)
Or choked by old books and boredom
As the consumptive by his own sputum . . .

You will understand, death has a different speech
Beyond Larnach's blind-eyed castle
When omens of the south sea burn
The cliff-edge bushes to bent bare sticks,
And you walking with wet shoes would find
A tuft of hair on the barbed wire,
Black horse turds in the grass:

[139]

There, when the dark tracks end, give out,
Death is a humour of life, a kind of home.

But down here, smoking in the sitting-room
After the art show, I have this one sense
Of the black kettles the settlers brought with them,
Powder-horns, cupboards of thin bone china,
Too close, too close for any comfort,

The corpse upstairs, all the white sheets tucked in,
A culture kept alive by the drug of death.

The Monument

Above the bush belt of green shrouded trees
And sepulchres of moss, up stairs of rock
And over spongy ground where tussock held
Late grains of snow, came to McKinnon's
Grey quartz phallus: a bushman's fancy
Primed in a damp bunk when the stag roars
And the crag wind uncovers with blue fingers
Bare Mount Elizabeth.
                              Who added that
Irrelevant cross? It was a hard climb
And we sat half an hour in the wedge-shaped hut
Drying our parkas, drinking hot coffee,
While keas banged outside.
                              You who lie
In dry beds, before you sleep
Or hold the friendly body of your wife,
Say a short prayer for mountaineers, deerstalkers,
Guides, explorers, men of the death-bound kind,
And for McKinnon, never washed ashore

By Lake Te Anau, 1892,
From ridge to ridge like a gun-dog driven by
The celibate angers of the northern mind.

At Wanaka

In the broken stone houses
Patched with pebbles, the miners lay

Down at night in their own coffins
But rose up in fine cold air to fossick

For the treasure buried under schist.
They went. I trudge on the lakeshore with

My son, my wife, my two nieces,
Our feet scuffing the yellow poplar leaves,

And all the tribes have died of thirst inside us.
The great launch roars out like a bus.

I remember how I walked to Luggate once
To get drunk, and waded lost

All night beside Mount Iron, through
The wrong fords under a mottled moon.

Getting pine cones for the black stove in the hut
I grant time lost, time gained, but nothing happens yet

Between the bought cribs and the lake outlet
To ease in us what lives, groans, yet turns to rock.

The Maori Jesus

I saw the Maori Jesus
Walking on Wellington Harbour.
He wore blue dungarees.
His beard and hair were long.
His breath smelt of mussels and paraoa.
When he smiled it looked like the dawn.
When he broke wind the little fishes trembled.
When he frowned the ground shook.
When he laughed everybody got drunk.

The Maori Jesus came on shore
And picked out his twelve disciples.
One cleaned toilets in the Railway Station;
His hands were scrubbed red to get the shit out of the pores.
One was a call-girl who turned it up for nothing.
One was a housewife who'd forgotten the Pill
And stuck her TV set in the rubbish can.
One was a little office clerk
Who'd tried to set fire to the Government Buildings.
Yes, and there were several others;
One was an old sad quean;
One was an alcoholic priest
Going slowly mad in a respectable parish.

The Maori Jesus said, 'Man,
From now on the sun will shine.'

He did no miracles;
He played the guitar sitting on the ground.

The first day he was arrested
For having no lawful means of support.

The second day he was beaten up by the cops
For telling a dee his house was not in order.
The third day he was charged with being a Maori
And given a month in Mount Crawford.
The fourth day he was sent to Porirua
For telling a screw the sun would stop rising.
The fifth day lasted seven years
While he worked in the asylum laundry
Never out of the steam.
The sixth day he told the head doctor,
'I am the Light in the Void;
I am who I am.'
The seventh day he was lobotomised;
The brain of God was cut in half.

On the eighth day the sun did not rise.
It didn't rise the day after.
God was neither alive nor dead.
The darkness of the Void,
Mountainous, mile-deep, civilised darkness
Sat on the earth from then till now.

A View from Duffy's Farm

The door is all but broken;
there's air and space inside, and
no one's likely to come in

with a telegraphed demand
for love, opinions, money,
because the high lip of ground

belonged once to Matt Duffy
and now to the wind that blows
this way over the south sea

carrying a whiff of ice,
the farm's first owner. The stove
rusty; the sink dry – my shoes

crunch the dirt that 'possums leave
in a farmhouse that's been long
abandoned. Yet one could live

quite well on almost nothing
in this place – some turnips from
a neighbour's field – gathering

mussels from the rocks . . . *Too grim,*
you think? I'd sew up the old
burst mattress in the bedroom

where Sarah slept . . . Sarah filled
a hedge-gap in Duffy's life,
perhaps more as a burnt child

than as a *de facto* wife:
drunk, she would give it away
to a man well heeled enough

to buy a drink. Quietly
with one belt on the earhole
Duffy the husband would say,

'Get in the truck!' Too simple . . .
Soon after she was buried,
on a bus he said, for all

to hear, spreading his arms wide
as if to grip some woman
of air – 'She died like a bird

in the frost' – No ghost, no one
will haunt here, because the door
is mercifully broken

as hearts, lives, rocks break. Down there
under twisted apple trees
that bear no fruit, a river

seems to bend the heads of grass
running invisibly through
the crooked gully. It flows

winter and summer down to
the beach, the township, as if
it ran from a hole in the clay

that Duffy had dug. *Belief*
is not the name for it . . . Let
the mind rest, the hard weight of

knowledge drop, as winter light
glitters on brown thistle-heads
outside the door: I cannot

promise more than this, the clods
divided by purgation
of frost, rustling autumn heads

of thistle – space, air, light in
a room whose door is broken.

The Muse

(to Louis Johnson)

The city spreads her nets; I'm out of it,
Neither hot nor cold; a moulting parrot;
The Muse won't visit . . .
Dried washing seems to flap

Round my ears – but, sipping tonic water
In the Shamrock bar this Friday,
One shape I saw, a drunk with unlaced shoe,
Rope of the hangman's vomit on his lip,

And he made exit up Maclaggan Street
To where a woman in a sack or shroud
Suffered the clouting winter of the town,
Too solid for the worm's hegemony
On a foul green-painted balcony –

And she to him – 'Husband, liar, drone,
What scissor cut the cord and brought you home?
Has the pub burnt down? . . .'
                              I think,
Johnson, it was the Muse, whom you and I
Unhinge by our civility.

The River

Nothing as broad as
the river can be seen
these days: it was dark
brown and deep
at corners where cattle graze,

and ran silently
by Mackenzie's cottage
where he made his boats
at its edge
choosing the thwarts cunningly

from bent manuka,
and we'd paddle upstream
past the ducks' island
in a dome
of daylong silence never

to be broken – I
break it now! The river
is foul weed and sludge
narrower
than I had supposed, fed by

a thousand drains: thus
the heart is twisted free
by thought's knife: the creek
runs to sea
finding its way without us.

Daughter

Daughter, when you were five
I was your Monster;
Leaving the pub, less than half-alive,
Hurtling in a taxi to the Play Centre –

You'd ride like a jockey up Messines Road,
Thumbs in my eyes, your bulky legs

On each side of my booze-filled head –
A red-suited penguin!

I'd spoon you out dollops of mushroom soup
Peel off the penguin skin, and tuck you down,
Uncap a bottle of White Horse, dredge up
My hangman cobbers from the town . . .

Five years later I'd wake at 2 a.m.
And see an upright ghost in a nightie
Standing beside my bed, mumbling
About a bad dream it had had –

You'd settle in with me like a bear cub
And wrap your arms halfway round my chest –
An atomic blast set off in the Sahara
Of my schizoid, never-quiet mind!

Incest? The quacks don't know their job.
I was your father,
I treated you like bone china,
Sent you sleepwalking back to your cot.

At seventeen your face is powder-white,
Your hair is a black dyed fountain,
Mooching round the house you slam doors
And wait to be rung up.

Why won't you work? That boil on your heel
Comes from going barefoot
In the wet streets. Last night
I dreamt I burnt a fish-skin coat

To turn you back into a human shape –
Wouldn't you yell! Yet I was glad

[148]

When you hoisted your private flag
Against the bourgeois gastanks – You're *my* daughter!

When I go in to wake you up
On a morning of ice and boredom,
You sleep with your mouth open
Like a soldier struck down in battle,

And I'm Narcissus bending over
The water face! From the edge of the pillow,
Red-veined, grape-black,
My own eye looks back.

To my Father in Spring

Father, the fishermen go
down to the rocks at twilight
when earth in the undertow

of silence is drowning, yet
they tread the bladdered weedbeds
as if death and life were but

the variation of tides –
while you in your garden shift
carefully the broken sods

to prop the daffodils left
after spring hail. You carry
a kerosene tin of soft

bread and mutton bones to the
jumping hens that lay their eggs
under the bushes slily –

[149]

not always firm on your legs
at eighty-four. Well, father,
in a world of bombs and drugs

you charm me still – no other
man is quite like you! That smile
like a low sun on water

tells of a cross to come. Shall
I eavesdrop when Job cries out
to the Rock of Israel?

No; but mourn the fishing net
hung up to dry, and walk with
you the short track to the gate

where crocuses lift the earth.

from *Words to Lay a Strong Ghost*
(after Catullus)

1 The Party

A kind of cave – still on the brandy,
And coming in from outside,
I didn't like it – the room like a tunnel
And everybody gassing in chairs –

Or count on finding you there, smiling
Like a stone Diana at
Egnatius' horse-laugh – not my business exactly
That he cleans his teeth with AJAX,

But he's the ugliest South Island con man
Who ever beat up a cripple . . .
Maleesh – the booze rolls back, madam;
I'm stuck here in the void

Looking at my journey's end –
Two breasts like towers – the same face
That brought Troy crashing
Down like a chicken coop – black wood and flames.

8 The Wound

It is not women only
Who lose themselves in the wound of love –
When Attis ruled by Cybele
Tore out his sex with a flint knife,

He became a girl. Blood fell
In flecks on the black forest soil –
So it was for me, Pyrrha,
And the wound will ache, aches now,

Though I hear the flute-players
And the rattling drum. To live in
Exile from the earth I came from,
Pub, bed, table, a fire of hot bluegum,

The boys in the bathing sheds playing cards –
It's hard to live on Mount Ida
Where frost bites the flesh
And the sun stabs at the roots of trees,

No longer a man – Ah! don't let
Your lion growl and run against me,
Cybele's daughter – I accept
Hard bondage, harder song!

12 The Rock

Arms of Promethean rock
Thrust out on either
Side of a bare white strip
Of wave-ridged sand – long before

I ever met you, Pyrrha,
The free world held me in its heart,
And half my grief is only
The grief of a child torn from the breast

Who remembers – who cannot forget
The shielding arms of a father,
Maybe Poseidon – out there
Where the waves never cease to break

In the calmest weather, there's a hump-backed
Jut of reef – we called it Lion Rock –
Growling with its wild white mane
As if it told us even then

Death is the one door out of the labyrinth!
Not your fault – to love, hate, die,
Is natural – as under quick sand-grains
The broken bladders lie.

13 The Flower

They've bricked up the arch, Pyrrha,
That used to lead into
Your flat on Castle Street – Lord, how
I'd pound the kerb for hours,

Turning this way and that
Outside it, like a hooked fish
Wanting the bait but not the barb –
Or else a magnetised needle!

Well; they've bricked it up – fair
Enough! You've sunk your roots in Australia,
And I'm free to write verses,
Grow old, be married, watch my children clutter

Their lives up . . . It was always a tomb,
That place of yours! I didn't know
Then how short life is – how few
The ones who really touch us

Right at the quick – I'm a successful
Man of letters, Pyrrha –
Utterly stupid! – a forty-year-old baby
Crying out for a lost nurse

Who never cared much. The principle
That should have made me tick went early
Half underground, as at the paddock's edge
You'll see in autumn some flower

(Let's say a dandelion)
Go under the farmer's boots

Like a faded sun
Cut with a spade.

At Queenstown

If you go up on a clear dry morning
You may find a few dog tracks in the frozen slush

Of the steep road, and round the next bend
The fir trees with their pollen-bearing candles,

Then at the top of the long hill
A chalet, not a monastery,

From which one looks down at the view:
The boats like water beetles,

Wooden motels and pine tree islands . . .
And later a full moon will take

Her own photograph of the Remarkables,
Black rock veined with August snow!

Now as the blind eye
In your brain struggles to open,

Admit: It's nice, but not quite human,
A dipsomaniac's limbo,

To sit like a sack of shit in a smart bar,
Never out of the death trance, looking at

The faceless terraced hills, the enormous blue
Vacant eyeball of the lake

That won't notice whether you go or stay
But only whether you have the money.

At the Franz Josef Glacier

The hot rust-coloured springs in the riverbed
Were dry, but a smell of sulphur

Haunted the trees along the faultline
Under the glacier face where the guide

Split with his ice axe a boulder of cunninghamite
And showed us the small rock garnets

Like blood drops. Brunner wrote of this country:
'March is a bad month to ford the rivers

On account of the moss that grows . . .' Yes, explorer,
Deerstalker, have to pass the needle's eye

To get where they are going. The griefs I carry
Are nothing. All men die. What sign

Can I leave on cairn or tree to tell
The next comer that my thoughts were human?

As red moss grows on the glacial stone,
Then thicker spores whose acid crumbles it

A little – then the seeds the birds may drop,
Making their own earth, sending down roots,

Cracking and rending the rock – so may my words
Give shade in a land that lacks a human heart.

At the Fox Glacier Hotel

One kind of love, a Tourist Bureau print
Of the Alps reflected in Lake Matheson

(Turned upside down it would look the same)
Smiles in the dining room, a lovely mirror

For any middle-aged Narcissus to drown in –
I'm peculiar; I don't want to fall upwards

Into the sky! Now, as the red-eyed tough
West Coast beer-drinkers climb into their trucks

And roar off between colonnades
Of mossed rimu, I sit for a while in the lounge

In front of a fire of end planks
And wait for bedtime with my wife and son,

Thinking about the huge ice torrent moving
Over bluffs and bowls of rock (some other

Kind of love) at the top of the valley –
How it might crack our public looking-glass

If it came down to us, jumping
A century in twenty minutes,

So that we saw, out of the same window
Upstairs where my underpants are hanging to dry,

Suddenly – no, not ourselves
Reflected, or a yellow petrol hoarding,

But the other love, yearning over our roofs
Black pinnacles and fangs of toppling ice.

Mother and Son

1

Blowflies dive-bomb the sitting-room
Table, this dry spring morning,

In my mother's house. As I did in my 'teens,
I listen again to the Roman-lettered clock

Chiming beside the statue of Gandhi
Striding towards God without any shadow

Along the mantelpiece. Time is a spokeless wheel.
Fantails have built a nest on the warm house wall

Among the passion vines. The male one lurks.
The female spreads her fan. Out in the rock garden

White-headed my mother weeds red polyanthus,
Anemone, Andean crocus,

And the gold and pearl trumpets called angels' tears.
Mother, I can't ever wholly belong

In your world. What if the dancing fantail
Should hatch tomorrow a dragon's egg?

Mother, in all our truces of the heart
I hear the pearl-white angels musically weeping.

2

There's more to it. Those wood-framed photographs
Also beside the clock, contain your doubtful angels,

My brother with hair diagonally brushed
Over his forehead, with a hot dark eye,

And myself, the baby blondish drowsing child
So very slow to move away from the womb!

Saddled and ridden to Iceland and back by the night-hag
He learnt early that prayers don't work, or work

After the need has gone. Mother, your son
Had gained a pass degree in Demonology

Before he was twelve – how else can you make a poet –
Yet we're at one in the Catholic Church.

I go out to meet you. Someone is burning weeds
Next door. The mother fantail flutters

Chirping with white eyebrows and white throat
On a branch of lawsoniana, and the darting

Father bird comes close when I whisper to him
With a susurrus of the tongue.

At Kuri Bush

A few days back I climbed the mound
Where the farmhouse had stood,

As green as any that the Maoris made
Along that coast. The fog was blowing

Through gates and up gullies
Hiding even the stems of cocksfoot grass

That had sprung up in place of
The sitting-room table and the small brass

Kerosene lamp my mother lighted
Every night, whose white wick would burn

Without changing colour. Somebody must have
Used the old brushwood fence for kindling

Twenty years ago. Outside it
My father stood when I was three or less,

Holding me up to look at
The gigantic rotating wheel of the stars

Whose time isn't ours. The mound yielded
No bones, no coins, but only

A chip of the fallen chimney
I put in the pocket of a damp coat

Before I bumbled back down to the road
With soaking trousers. That splinter of slate

Rubbed by keys and cloth like an amulet
Would hold me back if I tried to leave this island

For the streets of London or New York.
I hope one day they'll plant me in

The kind of hole they dig for horses
Under a hilltop cabbage tree

Not too far from the river that goes
Southwards to the always talking sea.

At Brighton Bay

Two concrete pillars whittled by the tide
Regard the meeting of the bay and river,

Useless as some authority
Whose function is evaded by the water

That flows in wandering channels. I'd go down
In winter, when rain spattered on the wide

Corrugated levels, my body not
My own, but gutted by

The opposites of sex and pain,
Like new-cut banks the river had gouged out

For me to kick down ritually –
That grotesque adolescent fury

We never grow beyond! Today I hoisted myself
Up the rock stair that's called Jacob's Ladder

This end of the bay, shoving through gorse, and stood
On the smooth edge of the flax-covered cliff

That tempted me to suicide
In those times. No squid-armed Venus rose

Out of the surf, but through the smashed gate
Of many winters, from the hurdling water

Came to my heart the invisible spirit
These words have given shape to.

The Bridge

Far up the creek I
often rode in
a rented canoe, my
paddles barely touching
the water's pollen dusted skin

where gorse-pods floated,
and slid under
the Black Bridge's rusted
bolts and tarry roof: there
one could make sherbert from water

with a matchbox full
of fizzing fine
powder. It tasted well,
nipping the tongue, in high
summer, when crickets chirred at noon

on each bush – lately
I went that way
not thinking, and saw the
bridge under fifty bull-
dozed yards of gravel and dry clay.

The Titan

The rock limbs of Prometheus
Lie twisted at the entrance of the bay;
Like corroded iron, overgrown
By barnacle, periwinkle and sea-lichen.
Children who bathe in that place clamber
Timidly over the ridges of his shoulder

Bull-wrinkled, spray-moistened, brushed by the kiss
Of the south wind that blows this way
Five hundred leagues from the breasts of the Andes
Over sterile beds of foam. Think:
It is a long time since he brought
The fire of Zeus to us,

Lightening our chaos. For many aeons
Hour by hour the sea vulture
Has been tearing at his guts. We had
All but forgotten his pain and his gift.
Calamity, time, deeply thwarted desire,
Bring us again to the place of the dark Titan,

And there are others. I cannot hear their voices.
I cannot see their faces. Not even the jingle
Of a stirrup, as they cross the river mouth
In late evening when sandflies rise
From rotted kelp. Only a pressure at
The fences of the mind. From clay mounds they gather
To share the Titan's blood with us.

To speak truly

To speak truly of this madness
It rose from the bare stones
On the sea shore, a cloud moving
At night among the mangroves,

Saying, 'Your young men must die
For no cause at all' – and in the foul bins

By moonlight, outside a newspaper office,
It juddered like a rat with small pin eyes
Heard, but not seen,
The sole thing awake in an empty town,

Squeaking, 'Whoever has a yellow face
Should be fried in petrol' – though later
It walked and resembled a man
And spoke of National Security
To workmen handling lathes and shovels
To a crowd of lunchtime clerks
To women in gardens or on cable cars
To children in an unbombed playground.

Who listened half believing it.

Home Pleasures

What can disturb us? The rent is paid.
The doctor certifies I am not insane;

Pulse as usual . . . Why does the demon come
Disguised as an angel of light? This evening,

Sitting late at a wood fire dusted with white
Thick funeral ash – yawning, talking, thinking,

I feel, like the boy's hand squeezing the giant's heart,
This wandering, useless, imageless pain

Connected hardly at all with the black wings
Unloading napalm on jungle villages . . .

Ten years ago I would have killed it quickly
With a teacupful of Bols gin,

But now I don't even say, 'Bugger!'
When clods and roots of trees break through the walls –

Recognising the grave will enter the house
Whether the door is shut or open.

Man, You Will Be Dust

At the crown of the rise an old church
Where the tukutuku work

Plaited by women's fingers, has split and dried,
Smelling of dust, and the wind is talking

Behind a flute-playing figure. What wind?
Quite different at night when they bring you

Not to another's grave but to your own!
Iron slabs of wood, the earth's black vulva

Trembling under rain – suddenly
You are an ancestor

[164]

Who never wished to be one – Death is a kind of life
As the Maori understood it,

And you who struggled all your life against it
Become a Maori – Stilt-walking

Pakeha, without words or money
You die, man!

Fitz Drives Home the Spigot

When you hammered the spigot in, Fitz,
With blow after blow of a mallet,
I felt the town shudder, very much afraid
That the drunk man would be king,

That the meticulous sorrow
Of widows and spinsters with small zip purses
Would be disregarded by drunken coalmen
Pissing against the hedge,

That daughters would go down singing in droves
To the oil tankers and open their white legs
To rough-handed rum-fed sailors, that well-bred sons
Would dive in your great barrel and happily drown,

That the black bones of Dionysus
Buried under the Fire Assurance Building
Had sprouted a million wild green vines
Cracking the pavements and the gravestones –

But fortunately you did not strike too hard!
The town shook once, and then regained its proper

Monotonous man-killing identity,
While you rubbed your belly and drank one pony beer.

Afternoon Walk

Along the bank of the Leith the five of us
Were walking that Sunday – first, Bubba
Trundled by Jean in his pushchair – then, you
In your brown slacks, John and I,

Each in his own afternoon – when we came up to
The bridge with its gate and chain, I thought
That the weirs were passionate almost beyond bearing,
That the wind swinging on ropes of willow

Over the water, was not sad at all,
But a voice or a breath from fields of high summer
Where harvesters were sweating – I could all but see
Their foreheads glisten, their back muscles tighten,

In the approval of the wind that washed
Equally over garden and gravestone
And our dry faces. Further on, a wet black dog
Came out of the duckpond shaking himself,

And in the Botanical House everything was green
Except for the turtle resting on a pipe,
His head just out of water –
My brother! – moving his flippers very gently,

Breathing slowly, avoiding any clash
With the enormous leaves of the banana palm
Above him, or the quick small fish below him
Darting over the mud – oh these afternoons

Dedicated to a neurasthenic God
Are hardly his or mine! If, later, when we settled
Down on the concrete rim of a dried-up pond,
And Bubba sat like a Buddha in the sandpit,

I lay down flat and rested, letting others talk,
While the wind kept moving in the macrocarpa
And the red galah birds were screeching
In wire cages – it was not to embarrass

Anybody – it was perhaps to make sure
My own heart was still beating
Stroke on stroke – because, as you know, my dear,
The world has to balance on a turtle's back.

At Rakiura

You may be sure no matron will ever row out
To get a child by sitting on the snouted rock

At the centre of the harbour. That phallic monster is
Of danger only to the seaplane

Taxi-ing in past the wooden lighthouse
Where muttonbirds squawk in their burrows

Growing fat for the Maori. No mitigation
Of the sense of being trapped by life

Will come to us from the shelves of the museum
Where they've stacked the junk of the early days,

Bullets, clay pipes, paper money,
The Lord's Prayer written on a seashell.

But honeymooners may sponge out a quarrel
With a kiss that gathers half its meaning

From beaches where the surf bangs over
Like the cracking of a two-mile-long flax whip,

And we who are older look at the headstones of
The grim dead, as ignorant as ourselves,

Those whom the cold Strait or whisky killed,
And go back to the guesthouse to stretch out

And hear the chug of a generator
Or the monotonous rumble of the wind above

The high roof, not talking, just lying
And thinking of nothing on a sagging bed

That would extend (I imagine) an equal tolerance
To a paying guest or a moneyless suicide.

Winter River

Nothing is colder than this water in winter
when winds crack the lopped pines
on the domain bank and send cones
rolling down to the water . . .

Thick bare brown roots tangled
below the sod wall. The boys
and their girls would sit on Saturdays
in a fog of awkwardness and watch

the river run out to the bay.
Ah well – it's easy
to come back, more or less alive
inside one's own unbreakable

glass dome, a dying Martian,
and think about youth.
I never liked it much.
I did not venture

to touch the thick blonde matted curls
of those man-swallowing dolls, our big sisters.
I had no sister.
Their giggles made me tremble

and coast away to the bathing shed latrine
in itchy summer torpor,
furiously inventing a unicorn
who hated the metal of Venus.

Yet they weren't metal. Now
they sag on porches, in back rooms,
flabby as I am, and the river
carries a freight of floating pine cones.

Grandfather

Old and
bald-headed as a turtle,
I remember you,
grandfather, at the trembling kitchen range –

(all your hopes drawn in
to a pond where the light

flickered and gripped you from above,
your dead wife's love) –

so hot with the damper out
a match would flare
at a touch of its explosive tip
on the black glossy surface!

Ah yes – you'd take
the white bone chanter
down from its rack, finger it and play it
so sweetly, lightly, the wristbone of a man

hollow at each end, or so
I think of it, life measured
into a tube wound round
with bands of silver.

You'd caught the notes, you'd stolen them
long ago, sitting like a young
ferret in a flaxbush while your father
tried to teach the elder son.

He taught you then. A champion piper
you could never read a note,
you *were* the tune! It didn't
help you much

when the bailiffs were in,
and the butcher of God's Word
dragged you in half, much later,
so that you gave up smoking and whisky,

fell, rose, fell, rose, fell,
always a worry to your wife –

my looking-glass twin,
when the fumes were boiling in your head

on a black morning, the horses stamping
unfed, the manuka dripping
in gullies mortgaged to the hilt,
did you say '*I* am Hell'?

I salute whatever
burns, our brother Lucifer
raging! This I understand.
Never the unhurt quiet end.

The River

My brother started the boat engine
Tugging on a cord, and I steered

Upriver with the tide behind us
Close to the outlet of the gorge:

No problem, except when somebody's
Plastic leggings, floating under water,

Twisted round the propeller. That same afternoon,
Lying down flat after lunch, I heard

The river water slapping, and thought about
Three buried selves: child, adolescent,

The young unhappy married man
Who would have hated this place – ah well,

Space is what I love! The three selves dance
In the great eddy below the Taieri bridge,

And I am glad to leave them, sprinkling water
Over the embers that heated the Thermette,

Having at last interpreted the speech
Of the river – 'Does it matter? Does it matter?' –

And carrying like salt and fresh inside me
The opposing currents of my life and death.

The Wheel

We had drunk perhaps a gallon of whisky
At my friend's house at the beach near Kapiti
(He had left a wife like a young flowering branch
And plunged, being humble, into the body of a mistress
Whose brass eyes and brass hair could keep
The Furies at arm's length) – I rode back
To the town on the dusty tray of a truck
That morning under the uninhabited
Wheel of the sky that promised no sleep
Or silence to man in whose breast
The axle is planted.
                              I came down through a green
Tunnel of leaves to my own house,
And my wife standing in the doorway said –
'You have come back. How long will you stay?'
The wheel of the dead did not cease turning
That day or any day.

At Naseby

'Mountains are mothers' – I wrote
those three words in an MS
book, beside a new poem,
long ago with a pen cut
from a rooster feather, when
the earth and I were much less

compatible – living then
in a lean-to at the side
of a sun-dried-brick cottage
a yard or two up the road
where they've put a FOR SALE sign –
no bigger than a garage,

but it's the place that counts – I
must have been mad! There are no
mountains here; just the poplars
raining down orange leaves to
rot in ditches, and a spry
shop that sells bread, potatoes,

chutney, magazines – far off
on the skyline a small spoor
of hills, but nearer at hand
nothing apart from the moth-
bright family baches and
sod houses worn by weather

shapeless as graves, among which
water-courses ramble like
veins of memory. I'm not
haunted much, climbing the track

to the swimming-dam, by that
grim boy step by step at watch,

my judge below the larches,
his mind like a coiled spring wound
tight by dread and hope, a quill
tucked in his pocket – because
I have forgotten his wound,
and trudging towards nightfall

I find that whatever is
other than self sleeps now like
a wife at my elbow, with
rough breasts of stone, from whose kiss
I turn, so as not to break
the hymen of Sister Death.

Winter Sea

I remember, much too early
To see it clearly through the dark lens,
My grandmother among the roses
An old woman with red cheeks – and how she slowly built
A ball of silver paper to stand in the never-opened
Dust-proof cabinet below the painting of horses
Running away from lightning.
                              There was a smell
Of coldness in the house and a child could touch
The china jug and basin in the bedroom
Cold and rough to the fingers, or see without stooping
Beyond the veranda a blue cold garden
Through a pane of coloured glass.
                              No doubt her hands were warm.

She carried a sack of oatmeal on her back
Twelve miles, walking beside the breakers
From the town to her own gate. At least once it must have
    happened that a blinding sheet
Of spray rose from the winter waves to cover her.

I go down to the beach and watch the fishermen cast
Their lines out beyond the evening surf.
These men stow tackle in the boots of cars.
Their lead sinkers catch in the crevices of rocks.
No names. No ancestors. The sea stands
Upright like the walls of an empty grave.

Reflections at Lowburn Ferry

They take trucks on board for the river crossing.
Not always safe. It has been known to happen
That the ferry tipped and the truck slid back
Slowly into the Clutha with ten men cursing
And three men praying that the stuck
Cab door would shift. But the willows are green
Low down on the water. I've often thought that when
I finally flake, or a minute after, the gate will open
On this damned ferry. Very likely they won't have heard
Of Good Pope John. They will ask me why
I have no obol under my tongue,
Or a cent, or a penny — unless the price has risen —
And I will float in the mud like an old sad turd,
Never to live, never to die,
Wishing to Christ that Christ would come along,
Even the Protestant Christ, like Oscar Wilde when young,
To shake a tambourine with the souls in prison.

The Jar

Up in Auckland about twelve years ago
In Lowry's house – before the roof fell down
On Lowry's head – I'd bought a peter of wine
From the owner of a Dalmatian vineyard,
And carried it with me wherever I went –
Something to ease the jitters,
Something to have beside my bed in the morning –

And while some were nattering in the kitchen
And some were dancing down on the wooden floor
Of the middle room – half drunk, I held it up,
And saw what I had never even thought of –

On the curve of the wine jar Dionysus lying
Naked and asleep in a black boat,
With a beard like the waves of the sea – and out of his belly
A vine growing, vine of ether, vine of earth,
Vine of water – growing towards a sky
Blue as the veins on the inside of a woman's arm –

Black boat, white belly, curved blue sky
Holding us in its hands, as if Earth and Heaven
Were the friends of man, permanent friends –

A picture of what can't be, as I sat gripped by
The mad, heavy vine of sleep.

Winter Poem to my Wife

Because the fog is a curtain over the town
Because the lights are rare and few like virgins

Because the fire spits little sparks and weeps white resin,
Because I am a wooden husband,

You go away from me down to the roots of water
To find the spiny sea-egg
Whose yolk breaks molten in the mouth,
You go down to the sea gate
And gather the black pods of iron flax!

Because the trees are fur on an old hairy cat
Because the cars travel with windmills in their bellies
Because the houses are shaking their crumbling fists of mildew,
Because I am a warty husband,

You go away from me into the Maori church
To find an old bone flute
Playing by itself in the darkest corner
And the shark's tooth and the flounder
And the tears of the albatross!

I accept these journeys.

Because the wind has lost its powder keg
Because the frost has started to scythe the street
Because the moon is a blind wet crystal,
Because I am a silent husband,

You go away from me to the middle of the bush
To find a coat of stones and staples
Or the lifted hair of the hurricane
That tries to spin the sun in a new direction.
That's not a bad idea.

I accept my fate.

[177]

Discovery

1

Our mariners at early morning
landed on the beaches
that seemed an open book unmarked by a script.
Our chains and keels left the first wound.
The savages welcomed us
in well-built huts
with sea-food, drink, and sometimes their own daughters
whose hands were like the touch
of wind on water, a thing we had not guessed at.
Behind this a curious
austerity: their statues carved in pumice,
elongated; their songs for the dead;
regalia of wood and feathers.

2

A savage killed a sailor.

3

We landed a second time
protected by the ship's cannon
and there was much plunder. Their women
fled to the marshes inland
but most of the men stayed to fight us.
Spears. Muskets. They died shouting.
Our captain planted a cross
to mark the site of the event.

4

Now we have a port. The people are
Christianised. Our anthropologist
has been studying the cargo cult
among the hill tribes, recording
invaluable material on tape.
Certain diseases are endemic.
In twenty-nine museums
there are masks made of wood, shell, feathers,
reflecting an austerity
we do not ourselves possess.
Their glance is like a slow poison
intruding on our vacancy.

A Small Ode on Mixed Flatting
*Elicited by the decision of the Otago University
authorities to forbid this practice among students*

Dunedin nights are often cold
(I notice it as I grow old);
The south wind scourging from the Pole
Drives every rat to his own hole,
Lashing the drunks who wear thin shirts
And little girls in mini-skirts.
Leander, that Greek lad, was bold
To swim the Hellespont raging cold
To visit Hero in her tower
Just for an amorous half-hour,
And lay his wet brine-tangled head
Upon her pillow – Hush! The dead
Can get good housing – Thomas Bracken,
Smellie, McLeod, McColl, McCracken,

A thousand founding fathers lie
Well roofed against the howling sky
In mixed accommodation – Hush!
It is the living make us blush
Because the young have wicked hearts
And blood to swell their private parts.
To think of corpses pleases me;
They keep such perfect chastity.
O Dr Williams, you were right
To shove the lovers out of sight;
Now they can wander half the night
Through coffee house and street and park
And fidget in the dripping dark,
While we play Mozart and applaud
The angel with the flaming sword!
King Calvin in his grave will smile
To know we know that man is vile;
But Robert Burns, that sad old rip
From whom I got my Fellowship
Will grunt upon his rain-washed stone
Above the empty Octagon,
And say – 'O that I had the strength
To slip yon lassie half a length!
Apollo! Venus! Bless my ballocks!
Where are the games, the hugs, the frolics?
Are all you bastards melancholics?
Have you forgotten that your city
Was founded well in bastardry
And half your elders (God be thankit)
Were born the wrong side of the blanket?
You scholars, throw away your books
And learn your songs from lasses' looks
As I did once – ' Ah, well; it's grim;
But I will have to censor him.

He liked to call a spade a spade
And toss among the glum and staid
A poem like a hand grenade –
And I remember clearly how
(Truth is the only poet's vow)
When my spare tyre was half this size,
With drumming veins and bloodshot eyes
I blundered through the rain and sleet
To dip my wick in Castle Street,
Not on the footpath – no, in a flat,
With a sofa where I often sat,
Smoked, drank, cursed, in the company
Of a female student who unwisely
Did not mind but would pull the curtain
Over the window – And did a certain
Act occur? It did. It did.
As Byron wrote of Sennacherib –
'The Assyrian came down like a wolf on the fold
And his cohorts were gleaming in purple and gold' –
But now, at nearly forty-two,
An inmate of the social zoo,
Married, baptised, well heeled, well shod,
Almost on speaking terms with God,
I intend to save my moral bacon
By fencing the young from fornication!
Ah, Dr Williams, I agree
We need more walls at the Varsity;
The students who go double-flatting
With their she-catting and tom-catting
Won't ever get a pass in Latin;
The moral mainstay of the nation
Is careful, private masturbation;
A vaseline jar or a candle
Will drive away the stink of scandal!

The Golden Age will come again –
Those tall asthenic bird-like men
With spectacles and lecture notes,
Those girls with wool around their throats
Studying till their eyes are yellow
A new corrupt text of Othello,
Vaguely agnostic, rationalist,
A green banana in each fist
To signify the purity
Of educational ecstasy –
And, if they marry, they will live
By the Clinical Imperative:
A car, a fridge, a radiogram,
A clean well-fitted diaphragm,
Two-and-a-half children per
Family; to keep out thunder
Insurance policies for each;
A sad glad fortnight at the beach
Each year, when Mum and Dad will bitch
From some old half-forgotten itch –
Turn on the lights! – or else the gas!
If I kneel down like a stone at Mass
And wake my good wife with bad dreams,
And scribble verse on sordid themes,
At least I know man was not made
On the style of a slot-machine arcade –
Almost, it seems, the other day,
When Francis threw his coat away
And stood under the palace light
Naked in the Bishop's sight
To marry Lady Poverty
In folly and virginity,
The angels laughed – do they then weep
Tears of blood if two should sleep

Together and keep the cradle warm?
Each night of earth, though the wind storm,
Black land behind, white sea in front,
Leander swims the Hellespont;
To Hero's bed he enters cold;
And he will drown; and she grow old –
But what they tell each other there
You'll not find in a book anywhere.

To Mate With

To mate with the air is difficult –
That sinuous invisible creature
Blows hot, blows cold, rubbing her grit of pollen
On the bodies of ploughmen and mountaineers

Who itch and curse! To mate with a river
Or a filled-up miner's quarry, that pleases me;
My cold kind mother, Sister Water,
Has no comment, accepts whatever I am,

Yet one may think of tentacles
Reaching, searching from under the darkest ledge,
And not want to be married. To mate with rock
Is obvious, fatal, and what man was made for,

Whose heart of rock trembles like a magnet
For deserts, graves, any hole in the ground
Where he may hide from Zeus. To mate with fire
Is what the young want most, like salamanders

Weeping in solitary flame, embracing
Red-hot stoves, walking the lava crust

An inch away from fire. Then, my old gravedigger,
To mate with a woman is the choice

Containing all other kinds of death –
Fire, water, rock, and the airy succubus,
Without parable, without consolation
Except that each is the other's boulder and victim.

Tangi

(to my wife)

You had tied green leaves around your head;
I laced a green branch in my lapel.
On the concrete path to the meeting house
It was the women who cried out,

Calling and replying, the voice of those
Who have accepted death. And inside the door
(A thing unacceptable to the world we inhabit, in which
No one is allowed to speak of death)

The dead man was conqueror!
I saw him lying in the open boat
Of his own coffin, with shut eyes, winged moustache;
Though his widow was weeping, he was not,

And I knew for the first time the meaning of
The yellow woven tukutuku panels,
The shark's tooth, the flounder, the tears of the albatross
Understandable only when death is accepted

As the centre of life – The opening of a million doors!
The rush of canoes that carry through breaking waves

The dead and the living! – I was glad to be
Participant. I washed my hands before eating.

The Flame

My son sleeps above – my wife is sleeping also –
My son's room smells of the incense that he burns
Before the Buddha – as good a way as any
Of yoking the demons that rise at puberty,

Not demons, other selves. At 4 a.m. I still sit
Awake at the kitchen table
Like a Martian in a space suit
Drinking coffee and writing. In forty years

I haven't found a cure
For being human. I can't get drunk
Now as I used to, dowsing the flame with whisky;
I have to live and burn

Thinking of Christ – Christ, who is all men
Yet has to be discovered
By each on his own – not this morning
His blood only, but his resurrection,

Like the voice of the wind blowing on troubled waves,
Like hard buds of japonica,
Christ who is ointment, and for whom I carry
The incurable wound of life, and stand in the black flame.

The Instruments

If this were indeed the final night
High up on the hill, above the gold claims,
Where wet needles fall on the shoulders,
Where voices out of the ground compel
Pity and recognition – if this night were final,
A drawing down of blinds

Over the human face and the instruments of torture,
I could understand it.
                    But not yet; one must still go
Another journey to another place
Where without kisses, without the clasping of fingers,
The snake-haired women will appear
Naked, clothed in our own deformity,

And take us singly through the gate in the rock
To the paddock of the slavegirl Blandina,
To where the soul is broken or else becomes
A bird, born out of blood, another creature.

The Child

The child under the bones of my breast
Is not yet born –
Like a red log in the fire I fall apart;
My life is burning me up –

This is the pain that I was born for,
Desirable only because there is nothing else,
No fires, no rocks, no sea, no land,
No dreams to keep me barren –

What will the child be? Will he rise
Out of my belly with a crown of flames?
Will he wear a coat of rye bread? How can a man
Give birth, give suck to a child?

He will be a child of stone.

Cleaning up After the Party

To clean up after the party, emptying
Five ash-trays, washing the wooden plates,
Scouring the sink where someone has vomited,
Putting the screen up in front of the fire –

And afterwards to have a smoke, go out
And see the low grey shapeless clouds move
Above the Phys. Ed. building – I can only
Describe it as a form of prayer,

Because it is necessary. Without it I would not
Understand the joy that father Jonah had
In the whale's belly – all but ashamed
To be cut off from human sadness,

Brawls, hopes, and the sexual rigmarole,
So quietly carried in the belly of what is not
That I would wish, if it were possible,
No other light, no other heaven.

The Fear of Change

If you and I were woken suddenly
By the drums of Revolution in the street –
Or suppose the door shot open, and there stood
Upright and singing a young bullfighter

With a skin of rough wine, offering to each of us
Death, sex, hope – or even just an
Earthquake, making the trees thrash, the roofs tumble,
Calling us loudly to consider God –

Let us admit, with no shame whatever,
We are not that kind of people;
We have learnt to weigh each word like an ounce of butter;
Our talent is for anger and monotony –

Therefore we will survive the singers,
The fighters, the so-called lovers – we will bury them
Regretfully, and spend a whole wet Sunday
Arguing whether the corpses were dressed in black or red.

The Sailor

North of the headland, holding the tiller,
You were aware of islands. Islands
Entering the eye as a burglar enters a room.

The terrible drunkard's longing took hold of you,
To swallow earth, to wrap oneself in leaves,
To stay if necessary ten years on one of those
Bush-covered lozenges of rock,
Beaten by spray, hauling up food in a bucket:

A desire to become luminous
Like stars looked at over hills in the rain.

Later, much later, a glow like fire on the clouds,
It was Auckland breathing in her sleep,
City of wounds, city of friends,
Where one must lift and carry the great boulders.

The dead have now become a part of us,
Speaking between our words, possessing all our dreams.
To be a sailor is to die of thirst.

The Seed-Givers

They have all gone.
             Night after night
Growing old in our clean houses, sighing before sleep.
We remember those who vanished. Into the earth they went
Or into air, like dust in front of a broom,
Conquered by a rational humane regime –
Women with black braided hair,
Walking ikons; men who stood like mountains . . .

Perhaps we never knew them.
I write these lines without hope
Clumsily at a table between night and morning
Uncertain who or what I am,
Yet all the same glad to be dispossessed
Of a longing and hunger for the city
That never stood on earth. Quietly the body contains
Like an old wallet, fluid, air and solid,
Enough to travel with.
             They bequeathed us
Pain. The soul must carry its new life,
Pain. At length for us the world is a useless tent.

Rhadamanthus

We got to that place by an unexpected tunnel
Where the cliff top sank in a V – behind a hummock
Under the green starlike leaves
Of some plant that clings to the earth.
Venus came over the sea to us
Lying (as so many do)
In one another's arms. She left us
Like shards of a dish the spade jars on.

To love at all is to be haunted
As stones are haunted by the ghost of water
Where a creek ran once.
                              I came after twenty years
To the same place. My bones cold and heavy.
It was not wise to come back.
Boulders and clay had fallen. From some cleft
A pigeon scuttered out. Above the place of love
The cliff was a high stone Rhadamanthus
Washed by the black froth of the sea.

Summer 1967

Summer brings out the girls in their green dresses
Whom the foolish might compare to daffodils,
Not seeing how a dead grandmother in each one governs her limbs,
Darkening the bright corolla, using her lips to speak through,
Or that a silver torque was woven out of
The roots of wet speargrass.
                              The young are mastered by the Dead.
Lacking cunning. But on the beaches, under the clean wind
That blows this way from the mountains of Peru,

Drunk with the wind and the silence, not moving an inch
As the surf-swimmers mount on yoked waves,
One can begin to shake with laughter,
Becoming oneself a metal Neptune.
                                    To want nothing is
The only possible freedom. But I prefer to think of
An afternoon spent drinking rum and cloves
In a little bar, just after the rain had started, in another time
Before we began to die – the taste of boredom on the tongue
Easily dissolving, and the lights coming on –
With what company? I forget.
                                    Where can we find the right
Herbs, drinks, bandages to cover
These lifelong intolerable wounds?
Herbs of oblivion, they lost their power to help us
The day that Aphrodite touched her mouth to ours.

The Millstones

I do not expect you to like it. Winter
Has found his way into the tunnels of the mind
And will not leave us.
                                Often between the millstones,
In a stranger's house, perhaps drunk,
One of us would remember
The lagoons and the water birds, sleep that came
Like the travelling of the tide under a boat's keel.

Endlessly in memory I followed the river
To the place it sprang from, among broom bushes
In a gully above the dam. Brother,
It taught me nothing but how to die;
The house is empty. In the paddock alongside it
On a tree one bitter shrunken apple.

It is the hour of ghosts.
                              Do not forget
The time between the millstones was a real time;
The battles were real, foul sweat, foul blood,
Though now the earth is trying to persuade us
We are children again. The gales of the south sea
Will hammer tonight on a shut window.

The Bluegums
(for Patric Carey)

The harsh Latin word, 'reality',
Has never suited us. It means this iron sea,
These hills cleft like an anvil, no chariots, only graves.
I suggest a compromise. So that, perhaps, if one man were to die,
Then later, after the funeral, when the powdered sponge-cake
      had been cut
And set on a cane table out on the veranda,
Then if his friend were talking even about sheep or football
You would hear continuously in the pauses between the words
The first man talking in another language
As the wind does between the branches of the great gumtrees –
Or as when a boat is being launched, the furrow lengthens on the sand,
And the waves steadily resound on the timbers
While somebody in an overcoat is watching –
Or if on a dead Sunday the key turns in the door
And another friend comes in, smiling a little,
Carrying a pack of cards and a bottle –
I ask no more than this. Those would be our poems;
Marks of the whip; a kind of punishment
For us who have drunk without hope the blood of Dionysus.

The Caryatids

Between night and morning but belonging to neither,
The hour when stars lean down to the earth with black flames
That the wise might use as a time for praying or writing letters:
We are not wise.
                        In a bedroom with a steel basin
And a suitcase, being insomniac,
One of us will finally beckon out of the wall
The mad boathouse-keeper with his box of photographs
Whom poets have called Eros.
                        Thinking about women –
And lighting one cigarette from another, while the white globe
Burns as it were on the roof of a cabin in a ship that carries us
      towards death
With no Brendan's isle to visit – we are driven to acknowledge
The ones that we loved best were the ones who broke us
Limb by limb – those natures uncorrupted by compassion
Except for a sparrow or a cat – they handled words like ploughshares –
As one lifted her face from a stunted field of rocks and grass,
Shouting – 'I will not!' – to her God; not to any man –
And one round-faced girl offered herself to be kissed, then wiped
      her mouth and said –
'You are – *nothing!* And one, a drunk voice on the telephone,
      muttering –
'The man I love has two phalluses!'
These are the deaf caryatids,
These and their companions, each with the same limbs
And a different soul, who taught us that the flesh is human
And superhuman, lifting up on bruised shoulders
Ton by ton, the pediment of night and day.

The Victim

The day had been cloudy. But in my dream there was no cloud.
Through some great dome of glass I saw the moon's disc
Standing over a hundred hills, with a shrivelling light
That glittered without distinction on limbs and statues.
It took my whole strength to raise my eyes
To that bright leprous face;
The moon had eaten half the land.

And when I woke I thought about various letters
Written to the popular press; the collecting of coins and ribbons
The conversation of corpses at one or two difficult parties.
I thought that the land of the living had grown too small and dry for us,
And remembered my uncle (who is now dead) bending in the shade
Of a ngaio hedge, turning the uneven wheel
Of a grindstone, pouring water, sharpening an axe,
While the thud of the wheel kept saying:
'The body dies;
The soul is not yet born.' This I understand.

But not that other light. Why should we abandon
The word, the hope, the root in the ground? I think it is time
They brought the Shunemite girl to old King David
To warm his bed. Among the blunt troops bred up to exterminate
    whatever lives,
Among the wire grilles, the burp guns and the bureaucratic files
Of a time that has freed its devils but never understood them –
The virgin Abishag – she who is the last treasure, walking without
    kerchief, daughter of the earth itself, –
Let her be brought to the King's bed
For him to get heat. This time things will be perhaps different.

The Doctrine

It was hope taught us to tell these lies on paper.
Scratch a poet and you will find
A small boy looking at his own face in water
Or an adolescent gripping imaginary lovers.
And the hope became real, not in action but in words,
Since words are more than nine-tenths of life.
We did not believe ourselves. Others believed us
Because they could not bear to live without some looking-glass.

'Are they real?' you ask – 'Did these things happen?'
My friend, I think of the soul as an amputee,
Sitting in a wheel-chair, perhaps in a sun-room
Reading letters, or in front of an open coal-range
Remembering a shearing gang – the bouts, the fights –
What we remember is never the truth;
And as for the body, what did it ever give us
But pain and limit? Freedom belongs to the mind.

That boy who went out and gazed at his face in the river
Was changed, they say, into a marvellous flower
Perpetually renewed in each Greek summer
Long after his tough companions had become old bones.
To act is to die. We ward off our death
With a murmuring of words.

Instruction

The austere angel of the wind
Was our first instructor. He came with a breath of seaweed,
The savour of red currants, or an armful of dry grass,
Blowing our way above gardens and graves.

Drunk with sunlight, we listened
To a monotonous language, not of the ear alone,
Explaining the forms of nature.
                                        Either on the wood of the back steps
Where wolf spiders jumped after flies, or under the ngaio leaves
Round the corner of the shed. We were children then. His voice
    has changed.
The shed and the house have been pulled down.
I watch the branches of the ngaio tree tremble,
Shaking drops of water onto my coat –
It could be rain; it could be tears –
Those whom I loved as much as I shall ever love
Have joined their voices to that of the wind –

Those whom I loved as much as I shall ever love
Whom the world has turned slowly into air or stone
As I also turn.
                        If blood drops rise
To the surface of the grey bark, one should not go away.
The words are becoming a little clearer.

Here

Here where the creek runs out between two rocks
And the surf can be heard a mile inland,
And the toetoe hide the nests of a hundred birds,
And the logs lie in the swamp like the bones of giants,
And weed is rotting in heaps on the surface of the lagoon,
And the cliff shuts out the sun even at midday,
And the track peters out in banks of seagrass –

Here, where only the wind moves,
I and my crooked shadow
Bring with us briefly the colour of identity and death.

[196]

Dunedin Morning

This humid morning half the town is waking
Like Jonah in the belly of the whale,

Uncertain whether the light is light or else
A delusion of the blood. I remember clearly

A friend who walked the yard in stockinged feet
Playing the bagpipes, thumbing the great drone,

With a sound like the wind in the macrocarpas. But now,
At this moment, the town climbs up from sleep,

Innocently, with a mild rumble of traffic,
As a drunkard wakes, for once, without remorse

And is glad to be alive. Surf on the beaches
This side of Black Head, like a dream remembered

For a while after waking, will haunt and comfort
Those who go to factories, offices and libraries,

Putting on the daylight mask, the hard heavy
Face of wood or lead. A susurrus of wind is moving

The fallen leaves on the ground by the museum,
As the day begins, having its own eccentric shape

Which none of us will ever know completely.

Letter from the Mountains

There was a message. I have forgotten it.
There was a journey to make. It did not come to anything.
But these nights, my friend, under the iron roof
Of this old rabbiters' hut where the traps
Are still hanging up on nails,
Lying in a dry bunk, I feel strangely at ease.
The true dreams, those longed-for strangers,
Begin to come to me through the gates of horn.

I will not explain them. But the city, all that other life
In which we crept sadly like animals
Through thickets of dark thorns, haunted by the moisture
    of women
And the rock of barren friendship, has now another shape.
Yes, I thank you. I saw you rise like a Triton,
A great reddish gourd of flesh,
From the sofa at that last party, while your mistress smiled
That perfect smile, and shout as if drowning –
'You are always –'
                                    Despair is the only gift;
When it is shared, it becomes a different thing; like rock, like water;
And so you also can share this emptiness with me.

Tears from faces of stone. They are our own tears.
Even if I had forgotten them
The mountain that has taken my being to itself
Would still hang over this hut, with the dead and the living
Twined in its crevasses. My door has forgotten how to shut.

The Garland

At times you are not present.
There are other times
(It could be walking up a path, on loose gravel, between lilac bushes,
Or driving a car late at night when the headlamps all of a sudden
    pick out the masts of a boat
From a river bank) – it may happen without premeditation
You inhabit my wrists, my arms and my shoulders,
As if you were a child, or a part of my own flesh,
The heaviest part.
It has very little to do with
The way you comb your hair, the words you might speak;
Perhaps it is not you. You only bring it about
As the wind makes pods of gorse shift on black creek water;
But the difficult moment is when I lie down beside my wife,
    switching off
The electric blanket, and between her body and mine
Your body is interposed. An invisible hernia. For this you can hardly
    be blamed,
Who simply put your arms round my neck
With a gesture of giving. But the garland is heavy. It makes my feet
Sink into concrete pavements as if into the new soil of a grave.

Bacchante

At the moment of apparent ease, the moment
When you take off your coat and stretch, and a wind shakes
The topmost leaves of a tree in the quadrangle –
When the fly that was buzzing has settled and begun to walk
On the flap of a torn-open envelope – one among many
That lie on the desk in your sun-drugged all-but-monastic cell –
At that moment, you will hear a small knock on the door

And one of the Bacchantes will enter,
The mouth set in a smile –
                    As a rearing horse
Plunges two ways, either down the cliff, or into the rock wall
That cannot split or hide it, so your heart will plunge
In aberration; and the white mouth will begin the chant
That ends only when the hours of your life are ripped and broken
On the black earth –
                    It was that shrill desire
For safety that won the attention of the Bacchantes,
Curling their lips, making their eyes glitter;
To wish for safety is the first drop of blood.

The Gale

The rubbed unpainted boards of the old church
Catch the sun a little, yawning at death and life
On the ridge below the cabbage tree – and if now the heavy wind
    should blow
Out of the south, scattering thought, making the leaves clatter,
I am glad of it.
                    Those who haunt us are useless to us,
And those who haunt us most are the most useless –
The face that wandered in the daytime dream,
The face, the straight brown body and the grip of hands,
That fantasy exploded like a light-bulb –
Because the soul by any face is robbed of silence, robbed of its own
    dimension,
Darkness, cold, depth, the cell of storm where now
Out at sea the boats are moving with throbbing engines
Against a proper gale.
                    I do not deny these chains
I have to carry; the chains of Eros; but turn to watch

The tide flood in at the river mouth,
Washing under the bridge, making the canoes float
Upside-down.
                    Freedom by death is the chosen element.
The black strings of kelp are riding on the tide's cold virile breast.

The Searchers

If one were to shout from the hollow of these cliffs
Toward the black sky – if one were to cry out suddenly
As a bird might hurtle in stupidity from the ledges
Toward the heart of the storm, as if the storm were peace –
What answer?
                    An echo descending, the ghost of a falling feather.
And we remember our fathers talking of this place,
How at such and such a rock the young man was drowned
Whose hair spread out like a halo, but when they dragged him
    into the boat
And turned him over, the nose and the lips had been eaten away;
How the woman tortured by love plunged into the blowhole
And was never found. We have come from elsewhere, choked by
    the tumour of life, wishing to be
Made over; and the spirits of the unwise will not haunt
Or trouble us. They are too much like ourselves.
It is perhaps that we search in the face of the storm for the features
    of a Father
Lost elsewhere; we discover a burnt tree-trunk or the bones of a dog;
And we are changing slowly into columns of gutted stone.

The Black Star

I do not know when exactly we saw the black star rise
Above the mountains and fields and the places where we
Were accustomed to gather. The colour of the earth was changed
As if by mildew. It was a calm day,
If I remember rightly, with a dry wind blowing over
The fruit-bearing plateau. Blossoms were falling that day
Onto our heads, into the wine
We had set out on tables. Then a child shouted,
'Look at the black star!'
                        We looked up and saw it,
A spot, a disc, a kind of hole through which
The blue water of the sky was being drained out;
Yet the sun was still there, the wind kept blowing,
The wine held its savour.
                  There were a few among us
Who wept, pierced themselves with thorns, and cried,
'Deliver us, Christ, from our sin!'
                    What sin?
Sins are bred in the marrow of the bones of men,
Painful no doubt, but the wisest learn to live with them.
I forgot to say some of us began to scatter paper money
On the greying earth. No one would stoop to pick it up.
The old people now keep close to their houses,
And the young have grown ungovernable – they run wild wearing masks
Of hair and stick and bone. The middle-aged are finding it
Tolerable; at least I do.
             As for the black star,
It whirls, it stands, it governs the day and the night,
And though we prefer not to speak about it,
We regard it in a sense as a new god – god or machine – we call it
The Equaliser.

The Seals

Two boys in jeans are gathering bits of wood,
Wading in gumboots at the sea's edge;

Two dogs plunge into the yellow surf
And come out shaking their coats and spraying sticky water

Everywhere. We ourselves are treading
On the rotted cork floats of fishermen

That crumble underfoot, or else we climb
Awkwardly along these spray-dark

Ledges, gripping the chains that rasp the hand,
Pegged to the rock with rusted pins of iron,

And look for the seals. The seals have gone
Some time ago to the ice-cap in the south.

We won't find them here; instead we will return
By car on the winding road beside the mudflats,

Trying to remember – I do not know the name
To call it by; but the seals I think might have told us what it was

Before they vanished into the great mirror
Where we also travel, not by the easy death

Of water, but by land, sun-struck, moon-blinded and
Pollutedly ourselves.

The Bargain

The rows of pea-plants in my neighbour's garden
Glisten with the dew. Paths of wet asphalt

Climb the near-by hill, under some kind of tree
Whose leaves topple in green waterfalls,

Leading very likely to a car-park or a junk-yard
But able to be thought of as the wandering track

That goes to a place where Brother Ass can bray
Without burdens. I can smoke, type letters, wind

The cuckoo clock, drink lukewarm coffee
In my scrubbed house – I have accepted God's bribe,

To be content with not being dead,
His singing eunuch – and my son who clatters

His hippie bells from room to room, my wife
Who makes pies out of buttered bread at the white range,

Even the grey cat blinking and curling its claws
In the armchair, are certain the bargain's a right one –

Yet if the prisoner ceased one day to sweat and rage
In his cell of jumping nerves and layered muscle,

Dreaming of wild women and guerrilla battles,
Bridges blown up, farewells in African hovels,

I would not be I, and the bargain useless,
For He would be cheated of the aroma of bitter blood

Spilt on the cross-tree, and I would have become
Simply the dead man hanging, the abdicated Jesus.

Poem Against Comfort
(for Peter)

To shift away from the mother's knees
Is hard – by which I mean these combs of sand
On a beach when the tide's out, or a funnel
Of broken rock rising above
The places where the fishermen cast their lines
A hundred times a day.
                              Kelp smell,
Sea smell, the brown bladdered womb
We finger and enter, yet cannot ever
Possess. And even if the comfort
Of a pebble placed in the mouth might hold back
The soul, that wild bird, from its flight
When the body shudders on a dented mattress,
It's hard to let go. But the night wind
And the day's drumbeat have told us
That any comfort is the cold blanket
Of a drunk in the dark. We have to strip
To the bone and beyond before the gate can open
And our silence be united both to what we leave
And to the dark centre of the sun.

The Serpent

The snake of lights in the North-East Valley
Curves uphill into a darkness where

Monument and TV tower will wait
The coming of either a nuclear deluge

Or the slow winding down of all our clocks.
I do not worry much. If in Biafra

They bury children under mounds of red dust
My dollars will arrive too late to change

The manner of their dying. Rather I
Must remember the phone call I promised to make

Yesterday – what was it about?
Did the number begin with five or seven

Or was it neither? My friend, perhaps the serpent
Has already eaten us.

Words for a Poet

Twenty years ago on a hangover morning
(Or was it afternoon?) we rode

Most ably, brother, in the small Austin
Through the green fabled

Land of drenched willows, river-flats and farms,
All of us acknowledge as the matrix

Of whatever grows in us. A broken springcart
Falling to pieces in a farmer's garage,

A church, a milkbar, any place or thing,
Meant understanding. Today in the same places

(You dead by drink) I grip the worn medal
Of friendship, and say – 'Old nurse, foul nurse,

'Why do you kill your children? Why do you treat
A man no better than a worn-out shoe?'

Epilogue for Ian

The subject is not to my liking,
How this one whispered – 'Bugger God' – and lay
Down dead in time to the famous tribal lament,

Or that one, having discovered the Vacuum, shrank
Rapidly to the shape of a little stone doll,
Labels that we invent and re-invent

For the same bottle. I can tell you, cousin,
Often I see my friends the suicides
Stabbing like needles through the cloth of life

To find the space behind it, or exploding
Like anxious migratory birds
That leave the pierhead empty and go north,

Counting them lucky but uncivil since
They did not want to share the fug with us in
This other death. But lately having heard

The great shout of judgement from your coffin
Standing on trestles in the asbestos chapel,
Preferring a bullet to a mother's kiss,

I admit I was wrong. Therefore, without argument,
While cars and relatives groan on gravel roads,
Sleep the black-bannered, the rock-undermining,

Sleep the contagious original sleep,
Now you have found the perfect girlfriend, now
The dark waters their reflections keep.

Séances
(for Colin Durning)

These mornings when the dead harass our lives
As children punish a dull parent,
With messages darker, wider, colder than
The crumbs of water on the sea's table,
It would be possible to let go the job
Painting or scaffolding the Tower of Babel,

Diver and dreamer, it would be easy
To cuddle up to the foetal envelope, pull
Over one's head the hummocked coverlet
Of trees and things. We have to put on instead
The space suit of money, the clean hair shirt,
That separate us from the lazy dead,

The irresponsible unborn. My brother,
I suggest we sit as usual in that café
Underground, a not too hard to bear
Grotto of the mind – talk, drink – where one can see
On certain days the stone-white face of Eurydice
Carrying in scorn her great gold helm of hair.

The Hero

All of us felt the tanks move in
With a grinding of treads in streets otherwise naked,

And the guns jutting out. It was easy to say –
'Killers! Killers of the green world!' –

Even to throw oneself down in front of the guns
And wait to be crushed. Some of us did that;

And the bespectacled young commander
Hesitated till his own men shot him,

And tossed his body over to our side
Of the invisible barricade. We wept,

Crowning his foreign head with flowers
For a hero's burial. But now, slowly,

Normality returns. The streets are cold.
The workday self that sided with the killers

Takes charge again, muttering – 'No love affair can last' –
And the hero's body rots to black bones and an agitator's myth.

The Bohemians

Led by a self-destroying sense
From homes with tons of junk they came
To wander and smile in the great city
To starve and die, to sleep or ride
In flexible arms of those companions

[209]

Who rose like off-white marble nymphs
From blankets and tree-roots, captivated by
The amateur heart, the hopeful will to die.

I admit, Colin, the fat brown comb that hangs
So full of myth on the gallery wall was born
In a rotting flat, from gin, sad friendship,
A shapeless tugging. But we forget: their city
Was the same boneless tiny necropolis
One sees from the window; their starvation
Was of the feelings, like our own. They did not
Differ from us except in their ambition,

Which for most, like thunder in the head, lasted
A year or two. I am astonished how
Mere ageing embalms with fatal significance
What at the time was a trivial drinking bout
Or something . . . Time does not run out;
It burns to the powder keg. And most became
Artefacts themselves, on ancient pillows
Propped, the nymph quite dead, the book unwritten.

Mining Town

The day the alluvial gold gave out
They left us these complicated diggings,
The plundered belly of the gravels,
A swivel gun, a shovel . . .
Where the cicada perches on black pipes
To indicate with a fiddler's stridulation
The blue self-hating void of summer.

The claims filled up with fine sludge and later
Some glittering death-regarding mirror

For a girl to drown in. It's all laid out
In the Mining Museum: faces, beards,
Glass bottles and the rusted iron cradle
In which the great nymph screamed and died. I mean,
Today an MP on the TV screen
Repeats the grandmother's prayer for wool, more wool
To wrap our parts with. In museums of the mind
We search out the Fracture, the second Fall,
A hundred graves, a worn-out clothing
On the dirty buttocks of the land.

And consider: Yes, it is another Sex
Resembling most a gradual suffocation
That binds even the youngest honeymooners
To fossick among the broom-bush canyons,
Drink beer and squash at the floodlit hotel,
And lie down mainly separate. I will
Define it more precisely: Say, as if
The groaning sound behind the mind stopped
And when we looked there we found the prisoner dead,
His mouth stuffed with rags. This Nobody,
Ourself, remains, a perfect citizen,
Tourist, voter, ice-cream-eater,
Unable ever to wake again.

The Eccentrics

It contents me to hear about them,
Not imitating their spectacular power
To bless the obstruction, master the idiot theorem:
Macpherson who rode the rapids with his arse
An inch above the water in a galloping
Canvas canoe, a lover of Scripture;

Faggott, the great drunk, who entered
A Methodist bunfight roaring like a bull
On all fours; Carmody who took pictures
Of clouds, clouds, clouds, with a tripod camera:
Giant augurs of the True, the Good, the Beautiful.

The Widow Life may weep to see them escape
The shape in the cellar, the choirboy's bellow of rape,
The whack of Caesar's whip, Queen Cybele's grip,
The excellent electrode: I condone it, Esmée,
For I admire these grey curmudgeons. They
Console me for the lover's bludgeon. May
St Ursula and the Eleven Thousand Virgins
Conduct them civilly to the Beatific Ballet.

Letter to Sam Hunt

Dear Sam, I thank you for your letter
And for the poem too, much better
To look at than the dreary words
I day by day excrete like turds
To help the Catholic bourgeoisie
To bear their own insanity;
And if in Paremata you
Should find a weta in your shoe,
Ugly, hard-shelled, with snapping jaws,
A Hitler who has lost his cause,
Don't hit it with a shovel – No,
Christen it JIM and let it go.

Though it may serve no good, in rhyme,
To look back on the fucking-time,
I do recall one evening, drunk

In Devonport on Dally plonk,
Endangering my balls and marriage
With someone's darling in a garage,
Upright and groaning, breaking eggs
Until the yolk ran down her legs –
One of the best of Venus' nuns,
A girl with tits like ack-ack guns
Who sighed and screwed and screwed and sighed
While her grim husband sat inside
The house and meditated death
For her and me with every breath,
Journalist, tombstone-maker, or
Some other kind of social whore.
Last year we met again and she
Not screwing sighed and looked at me,
A swaddled deathshead old and dry,
But there was life in that blue eye.

'Honey,' I said, 'You're thinking of
Another time when love was love.'
'You've struck it, brother,' she replied,
'But now I find the gap inside
Is cold and dark and hard to carry
And Buddha is the man I marry;
He teaches me that love is love
Only when it's past thinking of.'

Dear Sam, if you are twenty-two,
Why should I foist my gall on you?
The answer is that poets live
By a refusal to forgive
The mighty Bog of social shit
That has no use for sex or wit
Or art or hope, but simply is

Internally its own abyss;
At twenty-two or forty-one
You need your gumboots and a gun.

Sam Hunt, Sam Hunt, Sam Hunt, Sam Hunt,
The housewife with her oyster cunt
Has pissed upon what might have been
Lively, original and green,
The old pohutukawa tree
With hairy ballocks on its knee.
The Pill, the Rags, the Summer Sale,
Put Venus and her tribes in jail
Till every fuck's a coffin-nail;
Her husband, that sad pudding-head,
Will pull himself each night in bed
Softly, for fear he'll wake the Dead,
And teach his children how to lick
The Boss's arse and not be sick, –
Not that I blame the poor blind bitch
Who hoped that she would strike it rich
But saw her pretty flowers wilt,
Her cunt turn into a patchwork quilt
Her handsome Prince become a Frog
And drowned herself in the social bog.

But I must go my own way still
Across Death Brig and up Skull Hill
To learn the science of our grief
Conversing with the Impenitent Thief,
The one unique left-handed saint
Who knows why we must write and paint.
He teaches me that Sophocles
Heard in the thunder of Greek seas
On beaches grey with ambergris,

[214]

In the recoiling serpent hiss
A voice proclaiming to the land
That men are banks of broken sand,
And various other things that I
May put in plays before I die.

Dear Sam, this day as I came down
The steps that take me into town,
Rehearsing in my head these rhymes
That hold a mirror to the times,
A perfect omen crossed my track,
A garbage-eater, wild and black,
Pugnacious, paranoid and sly,
A tomcat with a boxer's eye
Dripping a gum of yellow pus,
I thought that he resembled us
Who may write poems well, with luck,
About the dolls we do not fuck
And hear the dark creek water flow
From a rock gate we do not know
Till we ourselves become that breach
And silence is our only speech.

To Patric Carey

From beaches grey with ambergris
The pressure of invention came,
Like waves that penetrate thin combs of sand,
That single, first, unknowable proposition
Published in theatres of stone
By actors roaring through great hollow masks
Not thunder, no, but the life of Aeschylus
Decaying to a hard wave-polished bone.

And still the mouths of actors vend
With Beckett, Brecht and Behan, what
The audiences know as well
As blood and semen, but forget,
That we are gaps in banks of broken sand:
Lucky the playwright then who keeps
After the public stoning and the praise,
Silence and one producer as a friend.

Valediction

The death-blue sluggish river in the South
Like veins on a dead man's arm . . . O you hills
Where I was born, the people at times were able
To light fires, to keep lamps burning
For their children to look at.
                                        There is more than one
Schoolhouse looking at itself in a lagoon
Where paradise ducks come down; but I must
Describe also a sadness like flint
Embedded in the eyes of brown-haired children.

It doesn't matter. The country is dragging
Chains of words, chains of money,
Decorated with a necklace of petrol bowsers
And waiting to be blessed by a good
Psychiatrist. My dreams do not go South.
Parents, grandparents, the fire you lighted
Under my arse will keep me moving
For another day at least. I will go North
Tomorrow like a slanting rainstorm.

Ballad of the Stonegut Sugar Works

Oh in the Stonegut Sugar Works
The floors are black with grime
As I found out when I worked there
Among the dirt and slime;
I think they must have built it
In Queen Victoria's time.

I had the job of hosing down
The hoick and sludge and grit
For the sweet grains of sugar dust
That had been lost in it
For the Company to boil again
And put it on your plate:

For all the sugar in the land
Goes through that dismal dump
And all the drains run through the works
Into a filthy sump,
And then they boil it up again
For the money's in each lump.

The bricks are held together by dirt
And the machines by rust
But I will work in any place
To earn myself a crust,
But work and never bow the head
As any grown man must.

And though along those slippery floors
A man might break a leg
And the foul stench of Diesel fumes
Blows through the packing shed

And men in clouds of char dust move
Like the animated dead,

To work beside your fellow men
Is good in the worst place,
To call a man your brother
And look him in the face,
And sweat and wash the sweat away
And joke at the world's disgrace.

And sweet on Auckland harbour
The waves roll in to land
Where you can sit at smoko
With the coal heaps close at hand
And watch the free white gulls a while
That on the jetty stand.

But the Clerk and the Slavedriver
Are birds of another kind,
For the clerk sits in his high glass cage
With money on his mind,
And the slavedriver down below
Can't call a slave a friend.

Instead they have (or nearly all)
The Company for a wife,
A strange kind of bedmate
That sucks away their life
On a little mad dirt track
Of chiselling and strife.

But work is work, and any man
Must learn to sweat a bit
And say politely, 'OK, mate,'

To a foreman's heavy wit,
And stir himself and only take
Five minutes for a shit.

But the sweat of work and the sweat of fear
Are different things to have;
The first is the sweat of a working-man
And the second of a slave.
And the sweat of fear turns any place
Into a living grave.

When the head chemist came to me
Dressed in his white coat
I thought he might give me a medal
For I had a swollen foot
Got by shovelling rock-hard sugar
Down a dirty chute.

But no: 'I hear your work's all right,'
The chemist said to me,
'But you took seven minutes
To go to the lavatory:
I timed it with my little watch
My mother gave to me.'

'Oh thank you, thank you,' I replied
'I hope your day goes well.'
I watched the cold shark in his eye
Circling for the kill;
I did not bow the head to him
And so he wished me ill.

The foreman took another tack,
He'd grin and joke with us,

But every day he had a tale
Of sorrow for the Boss;
I did not bow the head to him
And this became his cross.

And once as he climbed the ladder
I said (perhaps unkindly) –
'I'm here to work, not drop my tweeds
At the sight of a Boss; you see,
The thing is, I'm not married
To the Sugar Company.'

As for the Company Union,
It was a tired thing;
The Secretary and Manager
Each wore a wedding ring;
They would often walk together
Picking crocuses in spring.

You will guess I got the bullet,
And it was no surprise,
For the chemists from their cages
Looked down with vulture eyes
To see if they could spot a man
Buttoning up his flies.

It's hard to take your pay and go
Up the winding road
Because you speak to your brother man
And keep your head unbowed,
In a place where the dismal stink of fear
Hangs heavy as a cloud.

The men who sweep the floors are men
(My story here must end);
But the clerk and the slavedriver
Will never have a friend;
To shovel shit and eat it
Are different in the end.

Ballad of the Junkies and the Fuzz
(for Hoani)

1

Oh star I do not believe in, speak to me!
Star of the harbour night, wave after wave rising and falling
Under the bows of the Devonport ferry that carries a cargo of people
    home to their well-lit prisons,
Boys half lushed and girls in jeans or party dresses, older men looking
    vacantly at the black waves, women who do not show their souls
    in their eyes –
Star I do not believe in, shining also
In the rickety streets of Grafton where many gather
In a single house, sharing the kai, sharing the pain, sharing the drug
    perhaps, sharing the paranoia;
Bearded, barefoot or sandalled, coming out crippled from the bin
    or the clink.
(The windows painted black; yet the black paint was scraped off again) –
In order that the junkie rock may crack and flow with water
And the rainbow of aroha shine on each one's face
Because love is in the look, stronger than lush, and truth is in the mouth,
    better than kai –
Rain down your light, oh star of paradise!

Let the man the fuzz are hunting on the Domain
Kneel down and pray on sticks and wet grass –

His eyes are large as those of the owl on the rooftop
(Perhaps the pupils are dilated by amphetamine)

And the foul stink of the sweat of fear
Comes from his body where the capillaries have burst –

How can he sleep who has to watch the world
To see it is not strangled in the night

By his own sense of horror? Sometimes for a minute he dozes
And dreams he is the Golden One

The child crowned with flowers with a mother in a dark blue dress –
But wakes and remembers his job is to die

Either in the bin or with his head cracked open
By a stoker in a nightclub well loaded with lush –

'The wicked flee where no man pursues' –
To be so frightened he must be wicked –

His heart is thudding like a rapid drum
Telling him that soon the fuzz will arrive

With torches and full bellies to shift him to the clink
So that each honest man can sleep.

3

Baron Saturday, baron of the cemeteries, for whom they cut the
    black rooster's throat, whose altar is always a grave at the crossroads,
You have shifted, man, out of thin Haiti. Now you grow fat on the
    fears of five thousand junkies in Auckland.

How strange, man, to see those spruce and angry ghosts
Suddenly materialise
In an old house in the middle of the morning
When several are eating soup, one is playing the guitar, two are talking
    about nasturtium leaves,
And the others are snoring after an all-night party –
Suddenly you see them in the centre of the room,
The servants of the Zombie King –
Skorbul the football player with his brown moustache,
Krubble, who has a habit of crushing fingers in doors,
Drooble, who is glad to bang girls' heads on walls,
And one or two other clean-cut eager beagles
Young poltergeists squaring their shoulders, imitating the TV hero,
    hoping for a punch-up –
The fuzz are in the house.

'Would you like a coffee, Mr Skorbul?
'Naow.'
'A cup of soup then?'
'Naow. What y' bin doing round here?'

Star I do not believe in, let your tendrils of light grow
And out of them it may be we can make a vine ladder
To climb back to where God is, that high blue room in the sky.

4

On the wall at the bottom of my bed somebody has painted
A girl with a helmet of blue and white jungle flowers,
And the white centre of the largest bloom
Is the centre of the brain – I think she must be well stoned
On coke or morph, this heavy-lidded Lilith
Who was the first wife, the one whom Adam created
Out of a solitary imagination
When the world was very young – I do not mind at all
Having her watch me while I sleep.

5

It was necessary of course to invent the fuzz
To fence off the area of civilised coma
From the forces of revolt and lamentation
That rise around it, male and female
Ikons weeping tears of blood.

6

They have taken away Maori Johnny, the horsebreaker from
    Taumarunui. A keen pot smoker. He plucked for us the leaves
    of the tree of life. He knew also the secret of invisibility. One
    of the great kings of silence.
They have taken Blind Bob away to the bin. To cut his brain.
    Now he is for always a twelve-year child.
They have taken away young Vikki. She wrote to us on a bent bit
    of paper –

'ENTREAT ME NOT TO LEAVE THEE, OR TO RETURN
FROM FOLLOWING AFTER THEE, FOR WHITHER
THOU GOEST I WILL GO AND WHITHER THOU
LODGEST I   WILL LODGE. THY PEOPLE SHALL BE
MY PEOPLE AND THY GOD MY GOD . . .'

She will have her head shrunk and wear a poor dress and be touched
    by the Lesbian guards.
They have taken away Vanessa. Skorbul wanted to know all about
    her. She had breasts of fire and limbs like willow wands.
They have taken away Yancy. For a long time at the station Drooble
    kept banging her head on the wall. She lost her not yet born child.
They have taken Vic away. They broke his fingers. His mother said
    she knew Krubble was a good man.

7

Let the star shine. The star I do not believe in,
Star of the junkie night, flash in the head as the needle probes
    the vein,
Buddha Krishna Christ in one, making their own scene, smashing
    the wall of the dungeon,
Shouting – 'IT IS' – in the bright jail where the china ducks fly
    sideways up the wall
Beside the football pennants and the dead clock and the plastic rose
That covers a family coffin where many bones are buried
In a box of false peace – What do you see, woman,
When you look through the hole in the diamond ring? Is it a prince
    or a dwarf?
Is it a brown skull? The pain is greater than
Word or drug can cover – Star of agony shining
In the technological void. Do not shine again.

8

As the rain is falling, rain that is mercy rain that is memory falling
     on garden hospital and bridge,
A cat lies with his chick in a flat after midnight,
Her hair spread out on the pillow in the light of one oil lamp that
     burns in front of the Buddha on the shelf
And his arm tight around her shoulder
To keep away the cloud of paranoia
So that she can sleep.
Now that the methedrine is out of her blood, with no drug but
     her man there,
She sleeps as children sleep
Breathing very quietly and gently.

But every light on the ceiling of the room
Is the light of a squad car
And every noise of stopping and acceleration
Grinding on the metal of the road outside
Means for him the fuzz are at the door –
To break the locks, brother,
To tear down the wallpaper,
To empty the cupboards on to the carpet,
Looking for a single roach.

He kept his cool, man. But without a fix, man, that cat could not sleep.

9

Well, when we appointed the fuzz in place of God
It was a delicate decision.

The angels were astonished by their manners
Busting the diamond throne and looking there for pot.

[226]

There was a housewife whose name was Sally
Who thought it good one summer day to marry

Notwithstanding observation of her parents'
Wednesday and Saturday observance

Of the need not to procreate. Him and her together
Settled in a square place in good weather

And there was not for them a presence of neighbours
But the legal drugs that do soften our bad labours –

Librium and valium by a quack's prescription
Provided for much bread, some black bombers for slimming

And mandrax because the night time was lonely
When he could be absent with her by the boss's wish only –

The square eye in the corner of the money dungeon
As a substitute for lives of communication

And the noise box jabbering so loud and kind
To deaden the scream at the centre of the mind –

Him and her have had to pay down all but nothing
To get them one world-shaped enormous plush-lined coffin,

And of their two safe kids one is now in the bin
And the other has a cheese brain on account of methedrine –

Now Drooble bust their daughter and Krubble fronts their son
And the wing of paranoia does nail this country down.

Yet Sally and her man do frequently dispose
To converse to one another of the kindness of the fuzz.

10

Joanna is lying very fast asleep on a mattress in the smallest room,
A blanket over her naked body, one candle at her feet,
    the other burning down on the toe of an old boot that smoulders
    close to her face,
Her face freckled and white, her breathing very shallow on account of
    the ten Turinol her boyfriend gave her to balance the O.D.on starters.
A black filmy scarf flutters at the window, the wall at her head is a
    funeral black with one gold crucifix.
Tonight she will live or else die, the junkie princess lying on her chosen
    bed, two weeks out of the bin,
An inch away from death. To call a doctor would be to call the fuzz
To bust the house wide open. Her boyfriend and another woman
Are shooting junk in the front room, looking for a vein on the
    arm, cleaning the needle, while the music wails on gently from
    the player – cool, man, cool –
Their untroubled faces look inward to the dark Nirvana. The candle
    melts on the boot. The wind flutters the black scarf. Her face
    is white. Her breathing is very shallow. Either she will die or live.

11

The wing of the black angel is lying over
Us. Leaves had fallen when I met Vanessa
By the sportsground at Oakley. Brother Buddha,
I think love is being eaten by tigers
Inside or outside ourselves. That I accept.
It is time now to become *bodhisattva*.

Let us go together and knock on the doors of a million graves,
Walking on thorns and stones, telling the dead men –
Yourself, myself, Skorbul, Krubble,
And even that sad miscarriage Drooble –
That us each are persons and capable of love.

The Labyrinth
(for John Weir)

So many corridors, – so many lurches
On the uneven filthy floor
Daedalus made and then forgot, – 'What *right*
Have you to be here?' the demons thick as roaches
Whispering . . .
                Mind fixed on the Minotaur
I plugged onward like a camel that first night,
Thinking – 'Not long, brother, not long now!' –
But now so many nights have passed,
The problem is to think of him at all
And not of, say, the fact that I am lost,
Or the spark of light that fell upon my brow
From some high vault, – I sit down like a little girl
To play with my dolls, – sword, wallet and the god's great amulet
My father gave me.
              In the bullfights it was easy
(Though heroic no doubt) because their eyes, their eyes held me
To the agile task. Now I am a child
Frightened by falling water, by each nerve-pricking memory
Of things ill done, – but I do not forget
One thing, the thread, the invisible silk I hold
And shall hold till I die.
              I tell you, brother,
When I throw my arms around the Minotaur
Our silence will be pure as gold.

The Rocks

If I could I would go to the rocks at Mackenzie's corner
Where the river and the road both take a sharp turn
And the high broken rocks have given
Room for some thickets of green hard fruit,
The wild gooseberry. If I were to pluck and bite
One hard berry the taste might bring me

Out of the flame in which I burn,
And the touch of it on the tongue might bring back
The power of human speech. If the master of the flame
Would let me, I would gather from the tree at the gate
Where few go out, a leaf to cool my head,
And come back darkly at nightfall.

Like a wind among the houses
That shifts the spikes of grass but is not heard,
That does not need to turn a handle
Or knock. I would not wish to scandalise
Hearts I have loved, eyes that have answered mine,
Or the child asleep in her cot below the window

Who won't wake because the blind cord is swinging
But must not be touched by a burnt hand.
It would be better then to go by the outside way
Where the rocks are piled like the stones of Solomon's temple
And nobody will come, no footfall breaking
The silence of earth where, they tell us, the dawn can be seen.

from *Jerusalem Sonnets*
(Poems for Colin Durning)

If that Jerusalem which is unshakeable friendship with God
has not been established first in the heart, how can the objective
Jerusalem of communal charity be built so as not to fall?

I

The small grey cloudy louse that nests in my beard
Is not, as some have called it, 'a pearl of God' –

No, it is a fiery tormentor
Waking me at two a.m.

Or thereabouts, when the lights are still on
In the houses in the pa, to go across thick grass

Wet with rain, feet cold, to kneel
For an hour or two in front of the red flickering

Tabernacle light – what He sees inside
My meandering mind I can only guess –

A madman, a nobody, a raconteur
Whom He can joke with – 'Lord,' I ask Him,

'Do You or don't You expect me to put up with lice?'
His silent laugh still shakes the hills at dawn.

2

The bees that have been hiving above the church porch
Are some of them killed by the rain –

I see their dark bodies on the step
As I go in – but later on I hear

Plenty of them singing with what seems a virile joy
In the apple tree whose reddish blossoms fall

At the centre of the paddock – there's an old springcart,
Or at least two wheels and the shafts, upended

Below the tree – Elijah's chariot it could be, Colin,
Because my mind takes fire a little there

Thinking of the woman who is like a tree
Whom I need not name – clumsily gripping my beads,

While the bees drum overhead and the bouncing calves look at
A leather-jacketed madman set on fire by the wind.

3

A square picture of that old man of Ars
Whom the devil so rightly cursed as a potato-eater

Hangs on the wall not far from the foot of my bed –
Gently he smiles at me when I undo my belt

And begin to hit my back with the two brass rings
On the end of it – twenty strokes are more than enough –

Soon I climb wincing into my sleeping bag
And say to him – 'Old man, how can I,

'Smoking, eating grapefruit, hack down the wall of God?'
'By love,' he answers, 'by love, my dear one,

'By love alone' – and his hippie hairdo flutters
In a wind from beyond the stars, while I stretch out and dream

Of going with Yvette in a shaky aeroplane
Across a wide black gale-thrashed sea.

4

The high green hill I call Mount Calvary
Is only perhaps a hundred feet high

But it fills the kitchen window – man, today I puffed
Up the sheeptrack ridges and found three posts at the top

Conveniently disposed – behind that a grove of pines
With trunks like – well, I thought of rafters, roof trees

And ocean-going canoes, nor did I pick up one
Cone or stick, thinking – 'They belong to Te Tama

'In whose breast the world is asleep' – but when I came
Back down the gully a wild calf with a

Tubular protruding eye, white
Around its edges, jerking in the socket,

Ran from me – wisely, wisely,
Smelling the master of all who is never himself.

5

Man, my outdoor lavatory
Has taken me three days to build –

A trench cut deep into the clay,
Then four posts, some rusty fencing wire

And a great fort of bracken
Intertwined – a noble structure

Like the gardens of Babylon, made to hide
My defecation from the eyes of the nuns –

And this morning I found a fat green frog
Squatting in the trench – I lifted him out

Against his will and set him free,
But I am trapped in the ditch of ownership

Wondering if the next gale at night
Will flatten the whole ziggurat and leave me to shit naked.

6

The moon is a glittering disc above the poplars
And one cloud travelling low down

Moves above the house – but the empty house beyond,
Above me, over the hill's edge,

Knotted in bramble is what I fear,
Te whare kehua – love drives, yet I draw back

From going step by step in solitude
To the middle of the Maori night

Where dreams gather – those hard steps taken one by one
Lead out of all protection, and even a crucifix

[234]

Held in the palm of the hand will not fend off
Precisely that hour when the moon is a spirit

And the wounds of the soul open – to be is to die
The death of others, having loosened the safe coat of becoming.

7

My visitors have now departed,
Jill and Maori Johnny – they taught me to swear again

And brought me bad news of Boyle Crescent,
The junkies' pigeon-roost,

House of sorrow, house of love
To which my riderless soul night after night returns,

Neighing – 'Where are you?' It seems that somebody lit
A fire in the cellar, and two rooms were burnt out –

The wise tribe have left – Gipsy, Norma,
Yancy, Robert – the bones of my arms are aching

To hold them, my eyes want to look
On the streets of Grafton, where I was a king

For a little while – but the house of wood and straw
Is gone in smoke, and I am branded by that fire.

9

The crabs have returned – no creatures more communal,
Determined to be at one with their sad host,

[235]

They hang their egg-bags just above ground level
At the roots of hairs – or that is what I think

After investigation – perhaps bi-sexual,
With the double force of a mother's and a father's

Love they dig in like the troops in shellholes
Of World War One – so numerous a nation,

There's no danger, man, of genocide
Though I afflict them with pure Dettol

Time and again – I'd like to sign a truce –
'Have my moustache; and leave the rest free!'

But they have no Pope or King, Colin;
Anarchist, acephalous; they've got me stuffed!

11

One writes telling me I am her guiding light
And my poems her bible – on this cold morning

After mass I smoke one cigarette
And hear a magpie chatter in the paddock,

The image of Hatana – he bashes at the windows
In idiot spite, shouting – 'Pakeha! You can be

'The country's leading poet' – at the church I murmured, 'Tena koe',
To the oldest woman and she replied, 'Tena koe' –

Yet the red book is shut from which I should learn Maori
And these daft English words meander on,

How dark a light! Hatana, you have gripped me
Again by the balls; you sift and riddle my mind

On the rack of the middle world, and from my grave at length
A muddy spring of poems will gush out.

12

'Mother Mary Joseph Aubert, did you come here
To civilise the Maoris?' — 'No, my son,

'I came from my native France to these rough hills
Only to make them Christian' – 'Why then, mother,

'Are the corners of your mouth drawn down,
Why do you frown a little, why are your old hands folded

'In a rheumatic clench?' – 'Work, work;
Without work nobody gets to Heaven' –

'There's no work for the Maori in the towns' –
'Nonsense! There is always work, if one can

'Be tidy, chaste, well spoken' – 'The pa is all but empty,
Old woman, where you fought your fight

'And planted cherry trees – Pray for the converts' great-grandchildren
Who need drugs to sleep at night.'

13

It is not possible to sleep
As I did once in Grafton

[237]

Under the bright candles of a poor man's wall,
Under the delicate Japanese image

Of the Man dying whose arms embrace the night –
Lying curled in rough blankets, perhaps alone,

Perhaps not alone, with the great freedom
Of a river that runs in the dark towards its mouth –

Oh treasure of the poor, to be loved!
Arms and eyes I shall not see again –

It is not possible to sleep
The sleep of children, sweeter than marihuana,

Or to be loved so dearly as we have been loved,
With our weapons thrown down, for a breathing space.

14

I had lain down for sleep, man, when He called me
To go across the wet paddock

And burgle the dark church – you see, Colin, the nuns
Bolt the side door and I unbolt it

Like a timid thief – red light, moonlight
Mix together; steps from nowhere

Thud in the porch; a bee wakes up and buzzes;
The whole empty pa and the Maori dead

Are present – there I lie down cruciform
On the cold linoleum, a violator

Of God's decorum – and what has He to tell me?
'More stupid than a stone, what do you know

'Of love? Can you carry the weight of my Passion,
You old crab farmer?' I go back home in peace.

15

To give away cigarettes,
That's the hard one, Colin!

To live on rolled oats, raisins,
Potatoes, milk, raw cabbage,

It's even a pleasure – but I confess I need a smoke
More than I need a woman!

It's more like breathing – ever since I broached the guests' tobacco
(Along with the guests) I've been a doomed man!

Perhaps earlier yet – at six years old,
When I kept what I stole from my father in a rusty tin

Under the house, mixed with old rotted
Cabbage tree fibres – was it original virtue

Or original sin? I roll it now, and draw deep
The herb of darkness, preferring Nirvana to Heaven.

17

I went up barefoot to te whare kehua
This morning – but it seemed the earthquake god

Had been before me, represented by
Two young Maoris with a cunning bulldozer

That ripped up posts, earth, bramble, everything standing,
And left – well, the house

With its broken window, ghosts and lumber,
Severely out of date – I went in, treading

Carefully, to avoid a rotted kit, and knelt down
In front of the picture somebody had left to guard

The place – a cloudgazing pakeha Christ
With His heart in His hand, well felted against the weather –

And I said – 'Brother, when will your Maori church be built?
When will you hoist us all out of the graveyard?'

18

Yesterday I planted garlic,
Today, sunflowers – 'the non-essentials first'

Is a good motto – but these I planted in honour of
The Archangel Michael and my earthly friend,

Illingworth, Michael also, who gave me the seeds –
And they will turn their wild pure golden discs

Outside my bedroom, following Te Ra
Who carries fire for us in His terrible wings

(Heresy, man!) – and if He wanted only
For me to live and die in this old cottage,

It would be enough, for the angels who keep
The very stars in place resemble most

These green brides of the sun, hopelessly in love with
Their Master and Maker, drunkards of the sky.

21

Can this poor donkey ever carry Him
Into Hiruharama? Everything stands against it,

But that is the Rider's problem – on my kitchen shelf I keep
The square awkward tin that Agnes gave me

The day I left here going north,
A blind man walking – inside she put for me

Bread and cake and potted eel
To give me strength on that slow journey

To the mills of Hatana – now I am back here again;
The bread is gone, the eel is eaten,

And Hatana has written on the marrow of my bones
One kind of understanding – Agnes, I think, is out of it –

In Wanganui in her sister's house
Where the trees are cut down by the chainsaw and the ripsaw.

24

The kids here don't shout out, 'Jesus!'
Or, 'Hullo, Moses!' as they did in Auckland

When they saw my hair – these ones are too polite –
They call me Mr Baxter when they bring the milk;

I almost wish they didn't; but Sister has them well trained –
And soon she wants me to give them a talk about drugs;

What should I say? – 'Children, your mothers and your fathers
Get stoned on grog; in Auckland they get stoned on pot;

'It does no harm at all, as far as I know
From smoking it; but the big firms are unloading

'Pep pills for slimming, tablets for sleeping,
On the unlucky world – those ones can drive you mad –

'Money and prestige are worse drugs than morphine' –
That way I'd hit the target; but I doubt if the nuns would think it wise.

25

The brown river, te taniwha, flows on
Between his banks – he could even be on my side,

I suspect, if there is a side – there are still notches worn
In the cliffs downstream where they used to shove

The big canoes up; and just last week some men
Floated a ridge-pole down from an old pa

For the museum – he can also be
A brutal lover; they say he sucked under

A young girl once, and the place at the river-bend is named
After her tears – I accept that – I wait for

The taniwha in the heart to rise – when will that happen?
Is He dead or alive? A car goes by on the road

With an enormous slogan advertising
Rides for tourists on the jetboat at Pipiriki.

26

'Under a naked Master it does not fit well
The disciple to be too dainty' – so I paraphrase

The words of Bernard; for comfort, Colin, comfort
May kill the heart – so then, if the Dettol burns my jowls,

If the earth splits my fingers, if the wind is sharp
Blowing from banks of cloud as I go out

In a thin shirt, it is only to avoid
Being too dainty – the yogi Milarepa,

My son told me, lived for years on nettle soup
And his sister called him a fool – 'an ascetic hedonist',

Our theologians might comment – but how do they fight
The world and the flesh in their universities?

The naked Master who hangs above my door
Gave up, like old Milarepa, His bones to the bonfire.

27

Three dark buds for the Trinity
On one twig I found in the lining of my coat

Forgotten since I broke them from the tree
That grows opposite the RSA building

At the top of Vulcan Lane – there I would lay down my parka
On the grass and meditate, cross-legged; there was a girl

Who sat beside me there;
She would hold a blue flower at the centre of the bullring

While the twigs on the tree became black
And then slowly green again – she was young – if I had said,

'Have my coat; have my money' –
She would have gone away; but because I gave her nothing

She came again and again to share that nothing
Like a bird that nests in the open hand.

28

In a room full of smoke now that the stove is lit
The feeling of being on a space-ship bound for Mars

Is taking charge – the wing of the noonday demon,
I think, though he happens to visit me at night,

The hermit's familiar – What does he say? – something
Like this – 'You should be somewhere else, brother,

'Anywhere else; this stagnant life is bad,
Much too limited for a bloke of your talents

'Such as – well, you name them! – in the frame of modern life
You'd be better off doing – it doesn't matter what,

'As long as it isn't – well, digging in cow manure,
Eating, sleeping' – (he doesn't mention praying) –

'And as for that notion of yours of founding a tribe,
Hell, you're on your own here!' – I squash him like a weta with the shovel.

29

Our Lady shifted the demons; no need to talk about it;
It is her habit, lucid, warm,

Miraculous – but if you are consulted
One day, Colin, about my epitaph,

I suggest these words – 'He was too much troubled
By his own absurdity' – though I'd prefer – 'Hemi' –

And nothing else – today my new job
Is to disentangle the roots of the fourteen small

Green cabbage plants Sister Aquinas gave me
Wrapped in damp paper – one good use, man,

For the written word! – and put them in carefully
Where the beautiful loose earth is that crumbles to the blows

Of the grubber, and later give them a little water
When the sun cannot burn their delicate leaves.

30

If Ngati-Hiruharama turns out to be no more than
A child's dream in the night – well then,

I have a garden, a bed to lie on,
And various company – some clattering pigeons roost

At my back door, and when I meditate in the paddock
Under the apple tree two healthy dung-smeared pigs

Strike up a conversation, imagining, I think,
I am their benefactor – that should be quite enough

To keep the bowels moving and the mind thankful;
Yet when the sun rises my delusion hears him shout

Above the river fog – 'This is the hill fort
Of our God; it is called Hiruharama!

'The goat and the opossum will find a home
Among the rocks, and the river of joy will flow from it!'

33

Here in the morning there is no Vice Squad
To keep me on my toes – I'd cross myself once,

Say the Hail Holy Queen, then shamble out
To the kitchen to talk with Morgan – 'The house is filthy,

'Mr Baxter! That's not the way
To cure anybody' – 'Well, Mr Morgan,

'This is a kind of pakeha marae;
I'm only a lodger – you can see the one drug

'They've been using is alcohol' – Strubble would say nothing
But stroll round like a wound-up Spanish bull

While the kids climbed out of bed; I think he liked the place;
It felt like home to him – but here at 9 a.m.

There's just myself, the birds and Sister Aquinas
Knocking at the door with a bowl of dwarf beans.

34

I read it in the Maori primer,
'Ka timata te pupuhi o te hau' –

The wind began blowing; it blew for a century
Levelling by the musket and the law

Ten thousand meeting houses – there are two of them in the pa,
Neither one used; the mice and the spiders meet there;

And the tapu mound where the heads of chiefs were burned
Will serve perhaps one day for a golf course – yet

Their children fear te taipo,
The bush demon; on that account

They keep the lights burning all night outside their houses –
What can this pakeha fog-eater do?

Nothing; nothing! Tribe of the wind,
You can have my flesh for kai, my blood to drink.

The Black Book Song

Fingers, toes, mouth and nose,
And whatever hangs between,
All are branches cut away
From the tree of knowledge, long legs,
Heavy with the unborn fruit;
Plant them and they will take root,
But the goose girl weeps to see
Her great pile of broken eggs.

Mortar for the Painter's hand
On the wheel of silence turning;
None have learnt to bear it yet.
Do forget. Don't forget.

In the raw clay early shown,
By a knob or by a cleft,
Tender and their very own,
What is hard and what is soft
All the timid children learn
Then they hide the fear away
Behind a fog till Judgement Day.

Lovers in their drug-dark swoon
On the rack of Eden dying
Still must fight against the sun
And the arrows of the moon;
Long legs, I can hear you crying.
I will shut the black book soon.

Like an odour from the ground,
Blood of saint or sweat of lover,
Like an apple from the branches

That the yellow wasp has found,
Like the shoving of a river,
When the rack and rope are over
All is locked inside the wound.

And the old man in his cottage
Wakes to hear the midnight whisper –
'Do not sleep, my love, again;
Now my flesh has gone for ever
On the rock the tears run down.
You must pay the boatman's freightage
On the cold unquiet river;
You must love till time is over
With the sorrow of a stone.'

Long legs, I can see the sun
At my window jumping in.
I'll go water with a can
Lettuce, garlic, chives and beans.
I can shut the black book now.

Song for Sakyamuni

1

Loose as the washed pants and blouses that flap
On the thin wire they've tied round the corner post of the veranda,

My words are no longer the words of Apollo
But the river in its high gorges, life and death together,

Or the river in its shallows, mud and broken timber –
The body is a wound, Sakyamuni said,

Covered with damp skin, oozing out foul juice
From seven orifices, the wound we must bandage each day

In order to act and live in the light of the *Dharma*,
And my wound is half my trouble – the other half

Is the folly of believing I am I
In spite of contradiction – How hard to stop imitating

That waterlogged bee I saw on a clover head this morning,
Clinging to its red petals while the winter rain crashed down!

2

A thread can stop the bird from rising
Just as well as a domed wire cage;

My loves, I grant, are all self-love,
Except for the love I cannot call my own,

The wind that moves in the branches of the tree
Without premeditation – Can the stomach never vomit up

Those broken bits of mushroom, the poisoned food of Yama? –
'I am, I am, I am

'A poet, a Catholic, a dry alcoholic,
A man of forty-four' – you, Jesus, you, Sakyamuni,

Help me out of the pit! No ladder is necessary;
Ladders are part of the pit – my brothers, when the minute comes,

You will not see me; I will have gone out through the crack in the rock
Like an old lizard – No more, no more, no more Becoming!

3

There was a man who lived at Jerusalem,
He had an old coat, he wore his toenails long,

The newspapers made up stories about him
To entertain the housewives – why couldn't he live

In the Kingdom of Anxiety like any other man
And go into his house like a rabbit to its burrow?

God was his problem; God and the universe;
He had, let us say, a problem of identity –

Now, if you go to the valley of Jerusalem,
You'll find that the silence is like any other silence,

You'll find that the river is like any other river,
You'll find that the rain is like any other rain,

But the old man has gone out of the picture,
Leaving an empty picture frame.

Winter Monologue

One has to die here on earth,
My beard has got the stink of the ground already,

The opossum thuds in the roof like a man dropping bricks,
My belly is content enough

With two cups of tea and two bits of cake
Wehe gave me today as I sat on her doorstep,

But the night comes like a hammer cracking on an anvil
And all nga mokai huddle in the big house,

Playing the guitar, lighting up the little stove,
Not finding fault – one has to die

In order to water the roots of the tree with blood,
Guts, nerves, brains – once I was a word-maker,

Now my bones are buried at Hiruharama.
But the bones talk, brother. They say – 'Winter burns us like black fire!'

Ah well, soon I will go up the hill
To where the drain and the ditch and the new pipe

Are tangled in the dark – How cold it is!
The plumber has laid on running water

From the spring above the road – water, water,
That has to flow in the furrows of the garden,

That has to wash dishes, pots, old muddy clothes,
That has to be added to porridge or coffee

Before we can eat or drink – water is the sign of God,
Common, indispensable, easy to overlook –

How cold it is! Death will kill the cold
With one last stab, they say, and bring us to the sun-bright fields
   of Canaan.

But I must stay outside till the last of nga mokai
Straggle in – time then to soak myself in the hot springs of Heaven!

The Ikons

Hard, heavy, slow, dark,
Or so I find them, the hands of Te Whaea

Teaching me to die. Some lightness will come later
When the heart has lost its unjust hope

For special treatment. Today I go with a bucket
Over the paddocks of young grass,

So delicate like fronds of maidenhair,
Looking for mushrooms. I find twelve of them,

Most of them little, and some eaten by maggots,
But they'll do to add to the soup. It's a long time now

Since the great ikons fell down,
God, Mary, home, sex, poetry,

Whatever one uses as a bridge
To cross the river that only has one beach,

And even one's name is a way of saying –
'This gap inside a coat' – the darkness I call God,

The darkness I call Te Whaea, how can they translate
The blue calm evening sky that a plane tunnels through

Like a little wasp, or the bucket in my hand,
Into something else? I go on looking

For mushrooms in the field, and the fist of longing
Punches my heart, until it is too dark to see.

In Praise of the Taniwha

Te Ra is on his throne; the girdle of clouds is lifting –
E koro, you who lie in your nest below the bridge,

In my old coat I wander out to walk on the river bank and praise the
    world Te Matua is making,
The ancient One, whose sign is that pure disc in the sky –

E koro, generation by generation you have seen your children come
To open their eyes, small and weak in the whares, amazed at the light,
    leaning by day on the warm breast

Of a Maori mother, then standing, shouting, playing
On the roads of the pa, under the high green trees, fig or black-shelled walnut,

Always within the circle of your love
Old uncle, atua, friend, father,

You hidden spirit, dragon of the river –
'He is like a crocodile,' the half-grown girl told me, upright, wide-eyed,
    herself like a young tree in leaf –

You have seen them sweat, weep, smile; you have seen them go to their graves –
Now the pa is all but empty, the children are few, one elder is left,

The men are scattered like seeds to look for work in the towns,
Some in the jails or the borstals, some in an office, some cut steel on a lathe,

Only the graves and the ghosts remain at Hiruharama
And the river that floods from the hills and the gorges, swollen with mud,
    carrying the dead and the green branch!

E koro, my friend Peter was able to catch eels
Beside your home where the water boils under the dragging willows,

Because his heart was pure, because he spoke to you
As a father and a friend – I too, old one,

Not knowing who I am or where my road is,
I stand on the worn-out bridge and ask you to protect us,

These pakeha hermit crabs who are climbing into the shell of the pa,
Some stupid, some wise, and the Maori souls among us

Who are salt in the porridge, yeast in the new bread –
E koro, our eyes are dark, our pain is great, we are sticks broken to
    light a bonfire,

Yet endlessly the water rises in the deep hole under the willows,
Moving, coiling, whirling, at the moment when the world is made,

And your sign is in our heart, – the shape of our lives together is
    your own shape, –
Therefore, great angel, bless us, bring us to Te Whaea, to the Mother
    of all men, to the Void and the Beginning, – only the very poor
    have eyes to see you.

Conversation in a Garden

In the garden beside the dry swimming pool
Behind the big house, I recite the Third

Joyful Mystery in the company of Anne
Who stands as high as my right tit. It is certainly

An affluent neighbourhood, and the sludge tanks of the town
Empty into the tidal river

So that whatever fish you happen to pull out
Will twist your gut with typhoid. If I took the liberty

Of pissing against the doors of the local gasworks
There would be thunder. Reverberations,

Let us say. The river runs to the sea
Swollen to its bank with weeping from the hills

For what was lost in the Land Wars. Anne is uncertain
Whether to go to Varsity in Hamilton,

The land of LSD, or head back with this
Hairy etcetera to a windowless hutch

At Jerusalem. I tell her that obedience
Is pleasing to God and suitable for a woman

Under seventeen. Her parents have no doubt
Concerning the best course. Nor have I.

There is no river where the typhoid bug
Has not established its delicate tyranny.

News from a Pacified Area

The day of anger after the holy night
Will bring down corpses from the broken hills

Rotating like rubber ducks. All corpses are the same.
These were villagers who preferred something

To something else, or had the lack of wisdom
Not to dig deeper than moles when men came

With gas and grenades. Death is a good master.
He pays us and does not expect us to learn

The difficult art of keeping sane. We heard
The raped girl yelling in the barn

And when their leader showed his head
It was our own troops. Her grandfather's dramatics

Were singularly useless. I have no interest
In bucking the odds. My sister who became

Different tells me you can grow fat as a hen
Scratching in the shadow of the guns. My father,

For the last time I put melons on your grave,
And promise – what? Vengeance? Hope?

To distinguish the assassin from the victim
Would take God's knowledge, and he is dead

Because he requires our love to keep him in life,
And love is not our talent. I have grown a face

Whitish and smooth, like new scar tissue, brother,
To hide the evidence I am no longer I.

Getting Stoned on the Night Air

The long night fills the streets with fog
And the garages are wind-blown tombs

Under the leaves of the plane trees where I run
Lifting and dropping my arms like a bird

This mad night, – so peaceful, so dark and so open,
That the sea might easily flow over the land

Or the hills crumble like sand into the river
Since the town is a bed where the young and the old sleep

In the sweetness of being, – man, I don't need any
LSD to open the gate in the head

That leads into a land where men are birds
And Tanemahuta plays games with his children

In whorls and spirals of greenness, – even yes, to buy
One bar of chocolate and one packet

Of Pall Mall cigarettes at the old man's hutch at 3 a.m.
And share them with a friend, – that's one way

To carry the world and its colours, to balance it
On shoulders that are immortal only because they love.

Morning in Jerusalem

A cloud above the range like a honeycomb
Slowly being built, is what I groove on

From the window of the smallest whare, –
While I scratch my legs for fleas

And hear the others shifting in their dreams, –
Pure and wild the cloudbank, but later

It will be red and black for rain
Sitting in drops on the round leaves

Of the vines that wrap the broken branches
On the river edge below the pa, –

Rain comes from the east, as I put on trousers
White with feathers from a bust mattress,

The same shirt as usual, and the coat
With holes in the elbows and leather cuffs

I got from the Maori Welfare Officer, –
A head full of mud, a festering foot,

Wet grassheads whipping my knees on the track to the cottage,
And this is Hiruharama, the dark

Crucible of the alchemist
Where what is not can marry what is, –

So they say, the visitors who leave me
To make bricks with blood for mortar.

Ballad of the Third Boobhead

In a rackrent house not far from Aro Street
    One dark morning
Four men sat with a bottle of wine at their feet,
    And the rain was falling.

The first man said, 'The Government's not my mother,
    I worked on the boats for twenty years
And all I've got to show for hard skippers and bad weather
    Is the price of five beers.'

The second man said, 'The screws and the magistrates
    Are wearing me down,

I've been in too many boobs and too many fights
      In too many towns.'

Then the third man said, 'I've not seen Jesus Christ,
      But if he came
To earth he should either have had a gun in his fist
      Or stopped the whole game.'

The fourth man reached for the bottle and said nothing
      But the light from the window
Showed like a graveyard lamp that his hands were shaking
      And his skin was like calico.

And the third man said, 'It will take more than talk
      To make this a country
Where the men who were treated like slaves will be able to work
      For other things than money.'

Then the four boobheads caught on the horns of the beast
      Saw on that dark morning
Above the town like lightning in the east
      The bones of Lenin shining.

Ballad of Pigeon Park

I walked out one morning
From Firetrap Castle
Through the streets of Wellington,
Aiming to square the circle

Of Jesus and Lenin,
And down at Pigeon Park
I watched the fat birds hopping
On the edge of the grass,

When a young man got up
From the bench beside me,
And then
He opened his mind to me, –

'The pigs are on my back,
I don't live on milk or honey,
At the Labour Bureau
There's no job and no money,

'My mother was an Islander,
My father was a boobhead,
If you've got no money
You might as well be dead.

'I've hands, eyes and feet,
I didn't drop from your arsehole,
Why can't you treat me
Like a living man?

'I went to a party
Out at Island Bay
Where the tables were loaded
With half a ton of cray, –

'I'd had no kai for a week
And my gut was empty,
When they saw I was a stranger
They rang the pigs to get me.

'That night I walked alone
On the hills above the harbour
Till the dawn came
Like a blood-red hammer

[261]

'And the atua told me
There could be a time
When a man would be able to go
Through your streets in peace,

'And Jesus will come in at
The door of your churches,
Crowned with green leaves, like Adam,
But only when the benches

'Are shoved back to the wall
And a space made there
With cushions, kai and blankets
For the poor.

'Then I lay down right here
In Pigeon Park
And fell like a stone into
The gap between the stars,

'And woke with one of the pigs
Shaking me by the shoulder, –
"Get up, you black cunt," he said,
"You can't snore off here!"

'I went on down the street
With twelve cents in my pocket,
Not enough, man,
For a cup of coffee,

'And the windows were loaded
With chicken and steak
Like the pictures I've seen
Of the bodies at Belsen.

'"Come in and buy,"
The shop signs said,
But if you've got no money
You might as well be dead.'

'I went to my girlfriend's house
But she had shifted,
And a lady I'd never seen
Met me in the kitchen

'And told me to get going
I said I didn't want a fuck, man,
I only needed
Somebody to sit beside.

'I carried my empty guts
Down to the harbour
And looked at the water
Full of oil and shit,

'Then I got drunk
And smashed a plate glass window
And when the fuzz came
I planted one of them,

'And one of their heavies
Worked me over in the cells
With a booting on the kidneys
And a knee in the balls,

'And the magistrate said,
"This kind of behaviour
Can't go on!" He lumbered me
With six months in Mount Crawford.

'Your town is the bible town
That sit on the waters,
In your main street a man
Costs less than a dollar, –

'The atua told me
You can't last for ever,
I will play my guitar
The day they burn you down.'

He Waiata mo Te Kare

1

Up here at the wharepuni
That star at the kitchen window
Mentions your name to me.

Clear and bright like running water
It glitters above the rim of the range,
You in Wellington,
I at Jerusalem,

Woman, it is my wish
Our bodies should be buried in the same grave.

2

To others my love is a plaited kono
Full or empty,
With chunks of riwai,
Meat that stuck to the stones.

To you my love is a pendant
Of inanga greenstone,
Too hard to bite,
Cut from a boulder underground.

You can put it in a box
Or wear it over your heart.

One day it will grow warm, –
One day it will tremble like a bed of rushes
And say to you with a man's tongue,
'Taku ngakau ki a koe!'

3

I have seen at evening
Two ducks fly down
To a pond together.

The whirring of their wings
Reminded me of you.

4

At the end of our lives
Te Atua will take pity
On the two whom he divided.

To the tribe he will give
Much talking, te pia and a loaded hangi

To you and me he will give
A whare by the seashore

[265]

Where you can look for crabs and kina
And I can watch the waves
And from time to time see your face
With no sadness,
Te Kare o Nga Wai.

5

No rafter paintings,
No grass-stalk panels,
No Maori mass,

Christ and his Mother
Are lively Italians
Leaning forward to bless,

No taniko band on her head,
No feather cloak on his shoulder,

No stairway to heaven,
No tears of the albatross.

Here at Jerusalem
After ninety years
Of bungled opportunities,
I prefer not to invite you
Into the pakeha church.

6

Waves wash on the beaches.
They leave a mark for only a minute.

[266]

Each grey hair in my beard
Is there because of a sin,

The mirror shows me
An old tuatara,
He porangi, he tutua,
Standing in his dusty coat.

I do not think you wanted
Some other man.

I have walked barefoot from the tail of the fish to the nose
To say these words.

7

Hilltop behind hilltop,
A mile of green pungas
In the grey afternoon
Bow their heads to the slanting spears of rain.

In the middle room of the wharepuni
Kat is playing the guitar, –
'Let it be! Let it be!'

Don brings home a goat draped round his shoulders.
Tonight we'll eat roasted liver.

One day, it is possible,
Hoani and Hilary might join me here
Tired of the merry-go-round.

E hine, the door is open,
There's a space beside me.

[267]

8

Those we knew when we were young,
None of them have stayed together,
All their marriages battered down like
By the winds of a terrible century.

I was a gloomy drunk.
You were a troubled woman.
Nobody would have given tuppence for our chances,
Yet our love did not turn to hate.

If you could fly this way, my bird,
One day before we both die,
I think you might find a branch to rest on.

I chose to live in a different way.

Today I cut the grass from the paths
With a new sickle,
Working till my hands were blistered.

I never wanted another wife.

9

Now I see you conquer age
As the prow of a canoe beats down
The plumes of Tangaroa.

You, straight-backed, a girl,
Your dark hair on your shoulders,
Lifting up our grandchild,

How you put them to shame,
All the flouncing girls!

Your face wears the marks of age
As a warrior his moko,
Double the beauty,
A soul like the great albatross

Who only nests in mid ocean
Under the eye of Te Ra.

You have broken the back of age.
I tremble to see it.

10

Taraiwa has sent us up a parcel of smoked eels
With skins like fine leather.
We steam them in the colander.
He tells us the heads are not for eating,

So I cut off two heads
And throw them out to Archibald,
The old tomcat. He growls as he eats
Simply because he's timid.

Earlier today I cut thistles
Under the trees in the graveyard,
And washed my hands afterwards,
Sprinkling the sickle with water.

That's the life I lead,
Simple as a stone,
And all that makes it less than good, Te Kare,
Is that you are not beside me.

[269]

from *Autumn Testament*

1

As I come down the hill from Toro Poutini's house
My feet are sore, being bare, on the sharp stones

And that is a suitable penance. The dust of the pa road
Is cool, though, and I can see

The axe of the moon shift down behind the trees
Very slowly. The red light from the windows

Of the church has a ghostly look, and in
This place ghosts are real. The bees are humming loudly

In moonlight in their old hive above the church door
Where I go in to kneel, and come out to make my way

Uphill past a startled horse who plunges in the paddock
Above the nunnery. Now there are one or two

Of the tribe back in the big house – What would you have me do.
King Jesus? Your games with me have turned me into a boulder.

2

Wahi Ngaro, the void from which all life comes,
Has given us these woven spider-cages

That tie together the high heads of grass,
A civilisation in each. A stick can rip the white silk,

But that is not what I will do, having learnt
With manhood mercy, if no other good,

Two thousand perhaps in the tribe of nga mokai
Scattered like seeds now in the bins and the jails

Or occupied at their various occasions
Inside the spider-cage of a common dream,

Drugs, work, money. Sian, Kat,
Don and Francie, here with me at home

In the wharepuni – One great white flower
Shakes in the wind, turning a blind head towards our veranda.

3

Now we are short of meat, but up the path
Don comes carrying a goat on his shoulders

And I am astonished. 'What do you know,' he asks me,
'About butchering?' 'Not a bloody thing!'

Yet tonight I read a book by Debray the revolutionary
At the table where two candles burn

In front of the crucified Hero Father Theodore gave us,
While Don plays the guitar and Kat is talking

And Francie takes a bath in the other room,
And the dinner was good – half a goat's heart, a kidney and one testicle,

With cabbage and soya beans. Out on the hills
The moreporks are calling with human voices,

As the pa people tell us, for someone about to die,
But that could be anybody. Tonight we have our peace.

4

Wahi Ngaro, the gap from which our prayers
Fall back like the toetoe arrows

Children shoot upwards – Wahi Ngaro,
The limitless, the silent, the black night sky

From which the church huddles like a woman
On her hillock of ground – into your wide arms

Travelling, I forget the name of God,
Yet I can hear the flies roam through the rooms

Now at midday, feel the wind that flutters
The hippie goddess picture somebody painted

On an old blind and nailed on the wall. I can see
The orange flowers withering in a milk bottle,

Taste my tobacco phlegm, touch, if I like, the great bronze Christ
Theodore put up, on the poles of a cross he cut and bound himself.

5

Wahi Ngaro, now the ego like a sentry
At the gate of the soul closes its eyelids

For a moment, as today when
A crowd of ducks rose flapping at the place

Above the rapids where I go to bathe
Naked, splashing the water on my thighs,

And later I walked barefoot over the smooth boulders,
Thinking, 'There need be no other Heaven

'Than this world' – but rain spat soon
Out of a purple cloud, and I hid under

The willow leaves and bramble, as Adam did
Once from the Father. I brought back for Francie

A sprig of wet wild mint
That should go well tomorrow with the potatoes.

6

The darkness of oneself returns
Now that the house is empty,

A sense of danger in the room half dark,
Half lighted, seen through a squarish doorway,

Sticky rings left by cups on the table,
Darkness, the flutter of a moth,

A table spread in a tomb for the dead to eat at, –
That's it, the Dead! —– 'Why did you pay

A visit to Toro at night? Night is the time for the morepork.'
Wehe told me today, as we sat down to

Fried Maori bread, meat and pickle,
We who will certainly each of us one day return

[273]

To our mother the grave. The darkness of oneself
Comes from knowing nothing can be possessed.

7

To wake up with a back sore from the hard mattress
In a borrowed sleeping bag

Lent me by Anne – it was her way, I think,
Of giving at the same time a daughter's

And a mother's embrace – friend, daughter, mother –
These kids have heart enough to nourish the dead world

Like David in his bed – to wake up and see
The sun, if not the light from behind the sun,

Glittering on the leaves beside the graveyard
Where some of them cleared the bramble and placed on the bare slab

A jam jar full of flowers – to wake is to lift up
Again on one's shoulder this curious world

Whose secret cannot be known by any of us
Until we enter Te Whiro's kingdom.

10

The mossgrown haloed cross that crowns this church
Is too bleak for the mind of old Odysseus

Coming home to his table of rock, surviving and not surviving
Storms, words, axes, and the fingers of women,

[274]

Or the mind of Maui, who climbed inside the body
Of his ancestress and died there. Those who ride up river

In cars or the jetboat, see that high cross lifted
Above the low roofs of Jerusalem,

And speak of Mother Aubert and the Catholic Mission,
But when I see the sun fall and the moon rise

Over the edge of the ranges, I know what I have heard –
'The thoughts of a man's mind are many and secret' –

To the grass of the graveyard or a woman's breast
We turn in our pain for absolution.

11

At times when I walk beside the budding figtree
Or on the round stones by the river,

I meet the face of my dead father
With one or two white bristles on his chin

The safety razor missed. When he was younger
He'd hold the cut-throat with the ivory handle

And bring it with one deft stroke down his jowl,
Leaving the smooth blue skin. 'Old man,' I say,

'Long loved by me, still loved by many,
Is there a chance your son will ever join you

'In the kingdom of the summer stars?' He leaves me
Without a word, but like a touch behind him,

Greener the bulge of fruit among the figleaves,
Hotter the bright eye of the noonday sun.

12

The wish to climb a ladder to the loft
Of God dies hard in us. The angels Jacob saw

Were not himself. Bramble is what grows best
Out of this man-scarred earth, and I don't chop it back

Till the fruit have ripened. Yesterday I picked one
And it was bitter in my mouth,

And all the ladder-climbing game is rubbish
Like semen tugged away for no good purpose

Between the blanket and the bed. I heard once
A priest rehearse the cause of his vocation,

'To love God, to serve man.' The ladder-rungs did not lessen
An ounce of his damnation by loneliness,

And Satan whistles to me, 'You! You again,
Old dog! Have you come to drop more dung at Jerusalem?'

13

That grove of pines I prayed so long among
For the first six months, have been cut down for firewood

Or to make the floorboards of houses in the suburbs
Where children get square eyes. A dollar a hundred feet

Seems too small a price to get
For those green candelabra of the Ascension

Whose flames were pollen, but now the grove is gone
I go instead barefoot on the bulldozed clay,

Thinking, 'The pines are Pharisees,
They shove their solemn tough-barked crowns to Heaven

'But nothing grows under them.' One day on that ripped hill,
If God desires it, there will be a house

With Maori rafters, and over its doorway painted these words:
'Te Wairua o Te Kare o Nga Wai.'

14

Soon I will go South to my nephew's wedding
To the quiet land I came from,

Where all the ancestors are underground
And my father now among them. On my mother's wall

The picture Theo Schoon once painted
Shows him as the Iron Duke

With lines around his chin and mouth
Carved by the ploughshare. So he did look

In the time when a Labour Government planted my brother
On the Hautu prison farm for five years

For walking in my father's footprint
And refusing to carry a gun. Now in my mother's house

The picture is an ikon. Father, is it easier to fight
The military machine, or the maggots of one's own heart?

16

Nobody can win that kind of battle,
I don't try it – for a month or two

At Macdonald Crescent it seemed we might be able
To twist the arm of the Public Works Department

And make them disgorge one old empty house,
But it came to nothing. The boys who sat for five hours in the
    Labour Bureau

And couldn't get the Benefit, went to clink as usual
For being out of work. I tried the Gandhian tactic

Of fasting on coffee and lemon juice
For twenty-five days. It didn't ruffle one single

Bureaucratic feather! With no grots, no light, no water,
We cooked our rice and spuds on the open fireplace

And remembered the words of Saint John of the Cross:
'Our bed of love is made among the lions' dens.'

17

In those times the fast had made me thin
Though today the spare tyre is back under my belt,

And I'd go down for a coffee at the Hungry Horse
At three a.m. when the drunks gather,

And the dark angel of the town
Would mutter, 'Man, there's no way out

'Of this labyrinth! I mean to grind your soul
And theirs, and spit you out like rotten cabbage' –

Then Sharon at the corner with five sailors
Ran across to me and held my hand –

'Hemi, I'm going to crack it for ten bucks
With each of them; that way I'll get fifty;

'I'll hate it' – Above the town flickered the wings
Of the blood-red dove of Armageddon.

18

Father Lenin, you understood the moment
When the soul is split clean, as a man with an axe

Will split four posts from one log of dry timber,
But then your muzhiks still had souls

That smelt the holy bread upon the altar
And knew their mother's name. The mask of money

Hides too well the wound we cannot touch,
And guns are no use to a boy with a needle

Whose world is a shrinking dome of glass
A drug from Hong Kong will splinter open

With a charging elephant on a yellow packet
For riding home to deep sleep. The dollar is the point of it,

Old Father Lenin, and your bones in the Red Square
Are clothed in roubles till the Resurrection.

20

Somebody in my dream was shaking a blanket
Sending a gust of wind with dust and fleas

Over my body – and when I woke,
In the dark room I saw a wavering shape

Like a vampire in a castle in the stories
I used to read as a boy. Whether or not it came

From the graveyard forty feet away
From the house corner, fear increases the strength

Of any kehua – so I crossed over and switched on the light,
Smoked a cigarette, chewed over a few pages

Of Peter Marin, and began to write this poem,
Since a man who'll die some day should hardly fear the dead,

And the tribe need a father who is afraid only
Of ceasing to love them well.

21

King Jesus, after a day or a week of bitching
I come back always to your bread and salt,

Because no other man, no other God,
Suffered our pains with us minute by minute

And asked us to die with him. Not even guilty,
This morning I say the Salve Regina

While the fog is shifting slowly out of the trees,
Fry four slices of bread and eat them,

Then sit down under the image that stood once
In a Dutch farmhouse, then in a room in Putaruru,

Now in this place. It is perhaps the nimbus
Of Theodore's thick body and solar heart

That clings to the bronze, bringing to mind
Abundant loaves and multiplying fishes.

24

The brown grass that Barry cut for us
With the new sickle, is lying in heaps

Between the house and the door of the pataka
Where we stuck our mattresses. Barry has gone

Perhaps to Oakley where they'll pump him full of drugs
And ask him the meaning of the tattoos on his arm –

'Dad; Love; Hate' – he used to sail like a swan
Through the middle of the Courtroom up to the dock,

His coat split above the buttocks,
Boots loud on the floor, his forelock hanging

Over one eye, then tossed back, a débutante
Under the gaze of his friends. The fuzz were

Ignorant lovers in that brain-smashing courtship
Where love words are swearwords and kisses are blows.

25

Richard will not come here, the shy one,
Wary as a crayfish whose feelers jut out

From a crevice in the rock. When he was thirteen,
In the maths class, his teacher used to stand him

In a wastepaper basket at the front of the room,
And once I heard the lawyer ask him,

'Can't you think of something better to do with your life?'
'No.' The face like a young stone mask: .

'Idiots have no opinions.'
I heard him breaking bottles in the street

The night Naomi turned him down;
Naomi was a mother who had found him

Too hard to carry. Yet he broke no windows.
It hurts me to watch the snaring of the unicorn.

26

I go up the road under the eye of Te Ra,
And a cicada flying gets tangled in my hair

Until I set him free. Just as I finish
The Mystery of the Crowning with Thorns,

Rex pulls up in his truck – 'The new overseer
Is a little Hitler . . . The gristle's gone from my hipbone,

'When I lie down in bed the bones pull
Out of their socket.' He drives on through the dust.

I keep him in mind through the Carrying of the Cross,
Then kneel for God's Death by the black plastic tank

Where troughs are stuck in the moss to catch
The meagre trickle of midsummer

That flows through the pipe to the house. It's cool up here
Under the green ribbed branches of the pungas.

27

When I stayed those three months at Macdonald Crescent
In the house of Lazarus, three tribes were living

In each of the storeys – on the ground floor, the drunks
Who came there when the White Lodge burnt down;

Above them, the boobheads; and scattered between the first
And second storey, the students who hoped to crack

The rock of education. The drunks are my own tribe.
One Sunday, the pubs being shut, they held a parliament

In the big front room – Lofty with his walking stick,
Phil the weeper, Taffy who never spoke much,

And one or two others – in conclave they sat, like granite columns
Their necks, like Tritons their faces,

Like tree-roots their bodies. Sober as Rhadamanthus
They judged the town and found it had already been judged.

29

I think the Lord on his axe-chopped cross
Is laughing as usual at my poems,

My solemn metaphors, my ladder-climbing dreams,
For he himself is incurably domestic,

A family man who never lifted a sword,
An only son with a difficult mother,

If you understand my thought. He has saddled me again
With the cares of a household, and no doubt

Has kept me away from Otaki
Because I'd spout nonsense, and wear my poverty

As a coat of vanity. Down at the Mass
Today, as Francie told me to, I took Communion

For her (and Siân as well) cursing gently
The joker who won't let me shuffle my own pack.

30

Simply for bowing one's head in a little matter,
Strange that so great a peace should come!

I find that the flower like a star beside the power pole
Is made up of thirty separate flower-heads,

Each one a different blossom – why, I can't say,
But the light of God shines out of them,

The delicate pure invisible light I have not
Seen since I left Grafton. In those days

I'd climb the hill on the Domain
Before dawn, when the leaves were cold as iron

Underfoot, and talk with the trees – this one
Thinking she was ugly in her narrow dress of bark,

That one a woman who'd had many children –
The tree nymphs – their great beauty made me tremble.

32

Life can be a hassle. Are you free of it, Monsignor,
While you dispute the changes of the liturgy

Or polish up your golf style? At one a.m.
Either in your house or my house

The soul may plunge into pain like a child who slides
Through the grass at the lip of a mine-shaft,

Therefore don't ask me, 'What do you mean by that statement
You made to the Weekly News?' – or – 'What precisely is

'Your relation to Sally X – ?' A man is a bubble
Sticking to the edge of a mighty big drainpipe!

Let us be content to play one game of chess,
Share a coffee and biscuit, let Christ work out the deficit, –

There were eight souls, they say, with Father Noah;
Neither you nor I might have made it to the gangplank.

34

At evening the sandflies would rise from the river
And bite our bare ankles where we waited

For a tug on the line. Peter had dug
A pit in the bank to throw the eels in,

And when we caught one he tossed it there
To twist like a snake, the slime on its body

Plastered with mud. 'Hemi, pray for a catch.'
'It's quiet on the water;

'God is here.' We caught two more,
And took the first one up to Kóro Rangi

In case he wanted a kai. One eel fed twelve people,
But Peter was a chef. Carl put five eels in the bath

And studied them with an elf's attention,
The way their fins moved, the way they intertwined.

36

This fine windy morning I think about
The leper lying beside the fruitstalls in Calcutta

[286]

Under the shade of the great bridge. The oil-stained bandages
Around his limbs, the flies moving slowly

In and out of his nostrils, over his eyelids;
That lion face of dark mahogany

Turned up its brow to the overlying cloud
Behind which Rahm might live, from which a few spots

Of rain aspersed the pavement. I threw some coins
Into his tin dish. The policeman, built like a Maori

Guarding the fruitstalls in his khaki shorts,
Said, 'They're no use to him.' But the man was not quite dead.

When he was younger he should have had a gun.
There or in Karori, the sickness is, not to be wanted.

38

Last night a grey nimbus round the moon,
Today the rain comes from the west;

The leaves on all the trees look greener,
Rangimotu is burning piles of dry grass in his garden,

The flames go up to the low heaven,
And Wehe shouts to him from the door of her kitchen,

'You, come in out of the rain!' He only smiles
And goes on raking. I carry up the hill

A milk bottle full of sauce, bread and a parcel of sausages;
I plug the jug in and wait for it to boil

While the girls lie in bed. 'I like the rain.'
'I like it too. Aren't you afraid, Hemi,

'Of catching the 'flu?' 'Not exactly.
It's only that – ' The rain comes down in a dense white curtain.

39

The centre of our dreaming is the cave
That the world translates as brothel. Margaret told me once

A dream she had, about a house
In a meadow by the sea, old and full of passages,

Upstair and downstair rooms where the tribe were sleeping,
And three great waves came out of the sea

And washed around the house and left it standing,
Though for a while they had hidden the sun and the moon.

There has to be, I think, some shelter,
A home, an all-but-God, an all-but-mother

In time and place, not just the abstract void
Of I looking for me. Around these walls

They dipped their hands in paint and left their handprints
As on the walls of caves the Magdalenian hunters.

40

Three tourists come out of the church and stand on the grass rim
Above the pa. One of them points

At the big hall roofed with new iron
And walled with plaster board, where the men who built the bridge

Cooked their meals and slept at night –
'That's where the hippies lived. They had to kick them out.'

'They couldn't do much harm in this place.'
Their eyes are lenses looking at the houses,

Five or six, two of them windowless,
And missing out the aroha. Their fantasies will never

Be shifted in a world that's built to turn
On Us and Them. An old fear grips my belly

When I hear the brassed-off voices of the executioners
Who may one day come to burn us out of our burrow.

42

The rata blooms explode, the bow-legged tomcat
Follows me up the track, nipping at my ankle,

The clematis spreads her trumpet, the grassheads rattle
Ripely, drily, and all this

In fidelity to death. Today when Father Te Awhitu
Put on the black gown with the silver cross,

It was the same story. The hard rind of the ego
Won't ever crack except to the teeth of Te Whiro,

That thin man who'll eat the stars. I can't say
It pleases me. In the corner I can hear now

The high whining of a mason fly
Who carries the spiders home to his house

As refrigerated meat. 'You bugger off,' he tells me,
'Your Christianity won't put an end to death.'

44

This testament, a thing of rags and patches,
Will end soon. I cannot say, like Villon,

'Pray for me and for yourselves,'
For this is another century. That poor man ate his lunch

With the corpses of streetboys hanging overhead
And was part owner of some kind of brothel,

But the harps and lutes of paradise on the church wall
Were just as real as the bogs of fire,

The burghers sweated in their high fur gowns,
The slaves lay down to sleep on a straw mattress,

And most of it made sense. As if God had opened
A crack in the rock of the world to let some daylight in,

Saying, 'Be poor like Me.' Our life is the one
We make in darkness for ourselves.

45

Tomorrow I'll go down to Wellington,
Hitching, if I'm lucky, a ride down the river road

Past the karaka trees and the town houses
That turn the river into the Wanganui ditch

With shit that floats upstream below the bridges
When the tide pushes home. I'll go then

Southward among the sad green farms
Where the sheep get more freedom than their masters,

Past beaches with the plumes of toetoe blowing
In a wind that only Maori kids on horses

Can bargain with, down, down the straight coast road
To the dream city, the old fat sow

Who smothers her children. I'll wear no diving suit
And sit cross-legged in a pub doorway.

46

After writing for an hour in the presbytery
I visit the church, that dark loft of God,

And make my way uphill. The grass is soaking my trousers,
The night dark, the rain falling out of the night,

And the old fears walk side by side with me,
Either the heavy thump of an apple

Hitting the ground, or the creaking of the trees,
Or the presence of two graveyards,

The new one at the house, the old one on the hill
That I have never entered. Heaven is light

And Hell is darkness, so the Christmen say,
But this dark is the belly of the whale

In which I, Jonah, have to make my journey
Till the fear has gone. Fear is the only enemy.

48

The spider crouching on the ledge above the sink
Resembles the tantric goddess,

At least as the Stone Age people saw her
And carved her on their dolmens. Therefore I don't kill her,

Though indeed there is a simpler reason,
Because she is small. Kehua, vampire, eight-eyed watcher

At the gate of the dead, little Arachne, I love you,
Though you hang your cobwebs up like dirty silk in the hall

And scuttle under the mattress. Remember I spared your children
In their cage of white cloth you made as an aerial castle,

And you yourself, today, on the window ledge.
Fear is the only enemy. Therefore when I die,

And you wait for my soul, you hefty as a king crab
At the door of the underworld, let me pass in peace.

Ferry from Lyttelton

These bare hills have their own non-human beauty,
A country made for angels, not for men,

And the slow bow wash of the ferry
Covers and uncovers the rocks

At the bottom of the cliffs. Always the feeling comes
That one might leap over the side

And sink in the cold water. Not, I think
A desire to kill oneself

But a longing to go back and rest
In the waters of the womb. So, brother,

Button up your coat against the night breeze
Or come and have some toast and coffee

At the curved bar in swivel chairs
Where the waiter is a friend of a friend of a friend.

Torso I

These are the days, brother, when they screw the handles
On to the coffin of young men and old women
Who have taken their own lives. I remember Paula's face,
Like a sick dog or cat, the cheekbones of the skull
Jutting through the flesh – 'Now Karl is dead
I cannot go on living' – and that bright one,
Weyburn, who shot himself with the twenty-two –

They have to lower them gently into the ground
Because the spirit may trouble us. These are the days,
My friend, when the great shark rises
In the water of the heart. The chestnuts under the tree
Are bursting like bombs. A girl had written on my chest
With an ink pencil – 'You are an old bastard' –

None of it matters. If God has forgotten us
One day he will remember. Harder than flames or ice
For a man to endure is the heavy waiting
For a doubtful word. If my limbs tremble
You will understand it. The gate in the rock
Is half open. Shut it or go through it.

Torso II

If you put your fingers even once on my eyelids
You will feel the pulse beating. These old houses catch
The night wind like a sail; they are ships on a black sea
Too deep for a man to measure;
Yet memory is both colourless and transparent;
It tells me I was alive once.
                                        It was our own hands
Put the knife through the rib-cage
And twisted it. That was hardly the problem,
Sister. It seemed we had been waiting too long
For the word of release, bang!
One great kick from a giant's boot
Overturning the bed, the stove and the card table,
To lift us out of all pretending.
                                        In the loveliest of mirrors
We are still ourselves. Now I begin to understand it,
The hunger for the Judgement some have spoken about,

How the soul desires God as a stone must fall
Into earth or water.
                              Nose, forehead, eyes,
You are indeed yourself. And when you sat reading
The Letter of St John, I saw that other face
Take charge of you. A great angel,
One I had never seen, held you in his grip.

These moments I do not understand
Yet I am glad of them. Long ago we lost
Whatever keeps the boat on an even keel;
Memento, gesture, word; all gone.

Letter to Peter Olds

1

So hard to focus the ball of the human eye
On our terrible Mother, that stone Medusa

Sitting on her hill of skulls – suicides, abortions,
Gang-splashes, bloodstained mattresses, a ton of empty pill bottles,

And whatever else the wind may blow in the doorway,
Including, one may hope, the tired dove

Of the human spirit, raped again and again in the skyway
By the mechanical hawk. So hard for us to praise

The century of Kali – since a poem has to celebrate
Its moment of origin. As yet I am only able

To smile a little, and say, 'Not yet, not yet, Mother!
You must wait till I have brought the right kind of sawblade

'To turn the top of my skull into a drinking-cup, –
Then begin! Things have to be done in the right order.'

2

It is unlikely that anybody walking down Castle Street
Will get a bullet in the head

From a Maori or Island man whose cousin was kicked to death
By a cop in Auckland. The students are safe with booze, books or pot;

Those love-hungry grasshoppers jumping in the long grass
Where my soul is lying now like a rusty slasher

Under the chestnut tree – Hell, no, they aren't safe!
Is death by paralysis a sweeter death

Than death by a bullet? No man has ever been able
To dodge what's written in code on the night sky

Over our heads – 'Adam, I love you. Stand
Up and walk!' The effort to walk upright

Must have been a hassle for our daddy, the chimpanzee,
And I still find it difficult in nineteen-seventy-two.

3

Peter, your Eagle Angel still haunts me at times,
Though I think he may be simply a cousin of Te Whiro,

Our bog-eyed uncle, maker of ghosts and graveyards;
At forty-five I can't expect any other

Communication than what is given
By a wasp wandering in and out of the open window,

Or the wind that shakes the tree above the pataka,
Or the noise of Greg chopping wood out on the veranda,

Or the face of Kathy smiling with soap on her hands
That broad tribal smile. The agents of

A paranoiac culture will one day come with kerosene
To burn us out of our burrow. Then will be the time to say,

'Brothers, I have expected you
For a long time. Do you want to share your pain with us?'

4

The revolution doesn't need guns;
It happens whenever a man arrested for being

Out of work, and booted into the meat wagon,
Begins to laugh instead of squaring his fists;

It happens whenever a screw in Paremoremo
Walks out of his job instead of standing and watching

Twenty men bumming a boy. It happens
When the owner of the restaurant sits down with a moneyless customer

To pass the time of day. It happened for me
Lately at Taumarunui, when I stood on the grass of the marae

Beside one kuia, and said to her,
'When I am beside you I know that the earth below

'My feet is our mother. It gives me a sense of peace.'
The revolution happens when the eyes begin to open at last.

5

The rain is falling, Peter, on the hill of pungas
And the light is still on in the middle room

At midday. The little flies that rustle on my collar
Mistake me, no doubt, for a parcel of dead meat.

They like my stringy hair. They rub my forelegs together,
Zoom away like rockets when I try to grab them,

And regard me as their whenua. Gregg, with a white feather
Tucked in his hatbrim, is tidying up the table,

Rubbing down the old leather with a bit of crumpled paper.
He uses a broom as well as any chick.

'Kua ara te ra o nga tangata' – where the Lord is nailed up
On the wall of this room, he has, I think, a triumphant posture,

But in my heart he suffers the slow erosion
Of time, pain and silence. One day the great sun will rise.

6

The two pens in the big new chook-pen at our door
Are regularly trodden by the rooster;

They don't like it, but it may mean eggs
Carrying the spark of a tribe of chickens,

More eggs, more chooks! At first I thought
The fat rooster had taken monastic vows,

But that was only because they'd chopped off his tail
To put him in his travelling box,

And he didn't like it. I sit down with a tired gut
In the middle room to write you these verses;

The flies are using my scalp for a bush picnic,
Jumping one another and shitting among the hair-roots,

And I don't like it. Brother, it is not the social circus
Troubles me most, but the lack of significant action.

7

Have a wank for me, on the grass beside the Varsity,
I mean, at that old place between the Gothic turrets

And the waters of the Leith. It's hard to make a jail-break,
Especially when the screws are more or less polite,

And there's kai laid on, and they let you sleep at night, –
Call it the Old Man's Home. Up here at Hiruharama,

When I climb the ladder to the upper bunk
Perhaps I am a tribal shaman

Climbing the tentpole to the country of the sky
So that the dead can use his voice, –

Does he find a woman there? Well, that could happen,
But mainly, I think, it is the love of friends

[299]

Plants the tentpole, builds the walls of the house,
And will outlast with luck the fires of Armageddon.

from *Five Sestinas*

3 *The Dark Welcome*

In the rains of winter the pa children
Go in gumboots on the wet grass. Two fantails clamber
On stems of bramble and flutter their wings
In front of me, indicating a visit
Or else a death. Below the wet marae
They wait in a transport shelter for the truck to come,

Bringing tobacco, pumpkins, salt. The kai will be welcome
To my hungry wandering children
Who drink at the springs of the marae
And find a Maori ladder to clamber
Up to the light. The cops rarely visit,
Only the fantails flutter their wings

Telling us about the dark angel's wings
Over a house to the north where a man has come
Back from Wellington, to make a quiet visit,
Brother to one of the local children,
Because the boss's scaffolding was too weak to clamber
Up and down, or else he dreamt of the marae

When the car was hitting a bend. Back to the marae
He comes, and the fantails flutter their wings,
And the children at the tangi will shout and clamber
Over trestles, with a noise of welcome,
And tears around the coffin for one of the grown-up children
Who comes to his mother's house on a visit,

Their town cousin, making a longer visit,
To join the old ones on the edge of the marae
Whose arms are bent to cradle their children
Even in death, as the pukeko's wings
Cover her young. The dark song of welcome
Will rise in the meeting house, like a tree where birds clamber,

Or the Jacob's-ladder where angels clamber
Up and down. Thus the dead can visit
The dreams and words of the living, and easily come
Back to shape the deeds of the marae,
Though rain falls to wet the fantail's wings
As if the earth were weeping for her children.

Into the same canoe my children clamber
From the wings of the iron hawk and the Vice Squad's visit
On the knees of the marae to wait for what may come.

Sestina of the River Road

I want to go up the river road
Even by starlight or moonlight
Or no light at all, past the Parakino bridge,
Past Atene where the tarseal ends,
Past Koroniti where cattle run in a paddock,
Past Operiki, the pa that was never taken,

Past Matahiwi, Ranana, till the last step is taken
And I can lie down at the end of the road
Like an old horse in his own paddock
Among the tribe of Te Hau. Then my heart will be light
To be in the place where the hard road ends
And my soul can walk the rainbow bridge

That binds earth to sky. In his cave below the bridge,
Where big eels can be taken
With the hinaki, and the ends
Of willow branches trail from the edge of the road
Onto the water, the dark one rises to the light,
The taniwha who guards the tribal paddock

And saves men from drowning. Down to Poutini's paddock
The goats come in winter, and trucks cross the bridge
In the glitter of evening light
Loaded with coils of wire, five dogs, and wood they have taken
From a rotten fence. On the bank above the road
At the marae my journey ends

Among the Maori houses. Indeed when my life ends
I hope they find room in the paddock
Beside the meeting house, to put my bones on a road
That goes to the Maori dead. A gap I cannot bridge,
Here in the town, like a makutu has taken
Strength from my body and robbed my soul of light,

Because this blind porangi gets his light
From Hiruharama. The darkness never ends
In Pharaoh's kingdom. God, since you have taken
Man's flesh, grant me a hut in the Maori paddock
To end my life in, with their kindness as my bridge,
Those friends who took me in from the road

Long ago. Their tears are the road of light
I need to bridge your darkness when the world ends.
To the paddock of Te Whiti let this man be taken.

In Times of Trouble among Nations

Through the porch window I watch the birds tumble
In a tree of yellow flowering mimosa

As the sun goes down in the pale spring sky
And the mobiles made by my friend Jane

Tinkle above my head. They are made like birds and suns
Out of some local clay

Moulded with the fingers. I remember how the Yogi
In the Tibetan village would sit in the graveyard

Juggling skulls and thigh bones, with a rope
Of entrails round his neck,

Because one has to understand
Whatever is. The sun goes down

And leaves a gap of darkness
Too fiery and cold for any man to live in.

The culture does not love its demons,
That at least is apparent – shootings, bombs, car crashes,

Or even the drip-fed drug of money
That keeps the patient quiet in his high blue bed –

But without our demons how could we exist?
We would have to look at the void!

Rasputin said, 'I learn from Mother Earth.'
He spent a month howling in a cellar,

Then told the Tsar, 'Don't send the peasants into war!
They have too much to suffer,

'The generals will get fat on stolen money,
There may be a Republic.'

Rasputin died. The tumbling birds have gone
From the mimosa. The branches look like black iron.

The Return

When I go among the trees, up the path you know well,
Among the red flowers and the green grave-mounds
The trees do not receive me. I think their quiet breasts
Have been told by the Father that I do not belong there
But in some crevice of the ground
Or a place where men are quick to kill each other,

Where knives flash out because of something said,
Or where the street women let down their thick brown hair
To cover the eyes of a stranger. I think, my sister,
There is no longer a place for me
Under the trees where we climbed as children,
Accepted by the sky, accepted by the earth,

Accepted by the bones of the ones who gave us life
Down through many loins. Sister, if I tell you –
'I have slain a man to my hurt' –
Do not believe it. Put both hands over my eyes
And I can imagine water or green leaves
Or the wind blowing across the fields of grass,

Though indeed I am shut out
From the peace of our Father. Tell me, little one,

That my body is strong, that my hands are clean,
That my heart has in it a seed of light,
Then let me come beside you and hide myself
In the darkness of the garden of the sorrow of your face.

The Tiredness of Me and Herakles
(a letter to Herman Gladwin)

1

I trapped the great boar,
A Jansenist priest in his lair.
His tusks were longer than the Auckland Harbour Bridge
His logic pure as the seafoam,
'All men are damned except myself.
The christly do not have erections.'
The occasion of our dispute was a teen-age chick
To whom I had written a poem.
Though he booted me out of his presbytery
We parted civilly enough.
I asked him for a conditional blessing.

2

The cleansing of the stables
Took twelve thousand tons of river water.
The horseshit had hardened in the stalls like concrete.
You couldn't shift it with a pick or shovel.
Ritualism, fetishism, moralism,
Simplicism, angelism, dualism,
Drayload after drayload went swirling out the door.
I was afraid nothing would be left.
But when the floor was wet and cool as limestone

I found wedged in a crack one iron crucifix
And a thin medal of Our Lady.

3

The sky met the earth
To the west of that marae.
Great trees hung over the meeting house.
The earth giant did not greet me gladly.
'Apples,' he grumbled, 'too many apples,
My troubles began with an apple.'
But he let me take the rigid weight
Of the firmament on the strap-hardened shoulder
I got as a city postman long ago.
The apple that he plucked from the oldest tree
Burned in his hand like a sun.

4

In the battle with the shield-bearing women
I got this wound that makes me limp a little,
An arrow lodged one centimetre
Above the right testicle.
They cut one breast off to draw back the bowstring,
The other breast they keep to feed their children.
'Pornographer,' they shouted, 'you have poisoned the wells!'
The dust rose on a desert whirlwind.
Their queen Hippolyta grew amorous
After defeat. I did not like her.
She smelt of dexedrine and cabbage water.

All day I ploughed with savage oxen
That snorted and farted like runaway tractors.
That was the labour involving the printed rubbish
Plain men use at evening to wrap up fish and oysters
Or at midday as a table cloth.
The king was gloomy when the paddock had been ploughed
Though the furrows lay like polished metal.
'You are in danger of becoming vain,' he said,
'With too much exposure by the mass media.'
I noticed that the summer flies
Had laid their eggs in his beard.

6

The bout with Death was a hard one.
He wore a black uniform.
'Why don't you cut your hair?' he asked me.
'Life is filth. I keep the world clean.'
He had come with a pure heart from morning Mass
For a work-out at the police gymnasium
Before supervising the cleaning of a cell
That had some blood and vomit on its wall.
We wrestled in a fog of greyness
Till the swastika pin fell out of his shirt.
I was glad when the boss man called it off.

7

This wet October night
In a house in Auckland

The horseleech's daughter
Is crying, 'Give! Give!'
I have given her my fingers.
I have given her my liver to eat.
I have given her my skull to use as a soup bowl.
The ones who come here stoned on LSD
Forget they had a convent education.
To kill the heads of the hydra
You need a clever branding iron.

8

Three times in twenty years
I have wept a few tears.
I prefer laughter
But it gives me a hernia.
Herman, you old yelling shouting foetus,
Some wisdom has trickled through the cracks in my egg.
The drizzling grief of the town is the swag I carry.
A fist fight would improve the score.
I do not take my compass from Lenin.
My people rarely laugh or weep.
The fear of being hated has turned them into rock.

9

Today I smashed a green hydrangea bush
With a walking stick
At the edge of somebody's private lawn.
Every leaf was the head of a friend.
The meat wagon did not come to the scene.
Five labours still to go.
I am tired already.

[Moss on plum branches]

Moss on plum branches and
A soft rain falling – no other house
Spread out its arms around me
As this has done – I go
From here with a gap inside me where a world
Has been plucked from my entrails – fire and
Food, flowers and faces
Painted on walls – the voices of two friends
Recalling the always present paradise
We enter and cannot remain in.

[A pair of sandals]

A pair of sandals, old black pants
And leather coat – I must go, my friends,
Into the dark, the cold, the first beginning
Where the ribs of the ancestor are the rafters
Of a meeting house – windows broken
And the floor white with bird dung – in there
The ghosts gather who will instruct me
And when the river fog rises
Te ra rite tonu te Atua –
The sun who is like the Lord
Will warm my bones, and his arrows
Will pierce to the centre of the shapeless clay of the mind.

Ode to Auckland

Auckland, you great arsehole,
Some things I like about you
Some things I cannot like.

I came to the Art School, carrying the paintings
Of an eighteen-year-old chick.
On the door of one room somebody had written 'Life'
But there was death inside it.

A skeleton hung there by a hook in its skull
Its ribs brown with earth, age, or varnish.
The statue of a Greek god lay on the floor
With his prick and balls knocked off by a chisel.
'Alison,' I said, 'they've buggered the god of death,
They've cut the balls off the god of love.
How can their art survive?'

'Roimata ua, roimata tangata –'
The tears of rain are falling,
Tears of rain, tears of men.

I went to Mass at Newman Hall,
Then visited the Varsity Cafeteria
With six Catholic acquaintances.
One wanted to show me the poems he had written,
One talked about the alternate society,
One wanted to convert the world,
One girl in glasses gave me the glad eye,
Another praised the pentecostal movement,
Another hoed into his plate of cheese and camel turds.

I said, 'Excuse me a minute, there's a Maori friend of mine,
If he doesn't get a place to crash tonight

The cops will pick him up for the four crimes
They dislike most in Auckland,
Not having a job,
Wearing old clothes,
Having long hair,
Above all, for being Maori.
When they shift him to the cells in the meat wagon
The last crime might earn him five punches in the gut.
Could any one of you give him a night's lodging?'

They were extremely sorry.
The bourgeois Christ began to blush on the Cross.
The Holy Spirit squawked and laid an egg.
One had landlord trouble,
One had to swot for exams,
One was already overcrowded,
One didn't know exactly,
One still wanted to show me the poems he had written,
And the last one still silently consumed his plate of camel turds.

I took the Maori lad to Keir Volkerling's place.
He slept on a mattress in the bathroom.
Keir was not a Christian, or a student.
He worked ten hours a day
Digging drains or mixing concrete
To support an average of twenty-five people
Who would otherwise have been in jail
For being out of work,
For wearing an old coat,
For having their hair down to their shoulders,
And above all, for the crime of being Maori.

Christianity has weakened my brain cells, brother,
I haven't got the fortitude of Keir Volkerling.

The Auckland Varsity gives me a pain in the rectum.
I am waiting for the day
When its wedding cake tower goes down in a pile of rubble
From a bomb planted by an intelligent boobhead
Or a not-so-intelligent Varsity radical.

The Auckland Art School gives me a pain in both my testicles.
They don't know the best of Illingworth.
They admire the worst of McCahon.
Why not burn the Art School down
And get some old houses and do a bit of painting
Either with a brush on the ceiling
Or with a brush on a bit of canvas?

I paid a visit to an old friend
Who used to write some good poems.
The door of his office was painted black and yellow,
The colour of the plague flag.

'Peter,' I asked him, 'could you spare me a dollar?'
He looked unhappy.
He was putting on some ceremonial robes
For a meeting of the University Council.
'I'm sorry, man,' I said,
'I didn't mean to interrupt you.'

Outside his office the wind rustled
Dead leaves on the concrete pavement.
I shook hands with an old moss-grown statue
And went barefoot down the road.

Auckland, even when I am well stoned
On a tab of LSD or on Indian grass
You still look to me like an elephant's arsehole

[312]

Surrounded with blue-black haemorrhoids.

The sound of the opening and shutting of bankbooks,
The thudding of refrigerator doors,
The ripsaw voices of Glen Eden mothers yelling at their children,
The chugging noise of masturbation from the bedrooms of the
        bourgeoisie,
The voices of dead teachers droning in dead classrooms,
The TV voice of Mr Muldoon,
The farting noise of the trucks that grind their way down Queen
        Street
Has drowned forever the song of Tangaroa on a thousand beaches,
The sound of the wind among the green volcanoes,
And the whisper of the human heart.

Boredom is the essence of your death,
I would take a trip to another town
Except that the other towns resemble you exactly.

How can I live in a country where the towns are made like coffins
And the rich are eating the flesh of the poor
Without even knowing it?

O Father Lenin, help us in our great need!
The people seem to enjoy building the pyramids.
Moses would get a mighty cold reception.
They'd kiss the arse of Pharaoh any day of the week

For a pat on the head and a dollar note.
At another time in another place
Among the Ngati-Whatua
When they brought the dead child into the meeting house

She opened her eyes and smiled.

[313]

A Glossary of Māori Words and Phrases

atua spirit

e particle used before proper name when addressing someone

hāngī earth oven, or, by common usage, a feast
Hātana Satan
he a, some
Hemi James
hinaki eel-trap
hine young woman
Hiruharama Jerusalem

inanga a pale translucent variety of greenstone, also whitebait

ka timata o te pupuhi o te hau the wind began blowing
kai food
Te Kare one of Jacquie Baxter's forenames
Te Kare o Ngā Wai Te Kare of the waters
kēhua ghost
kono woven food basket
koro uncle, grandfather, older relative
kua introductory word indicating past tense
kua ara te ra o tāngata the day of man's resurrection has come

mākutu spell; curse
Māui mythological Māori hero, one of whose exploits was to try to
    kill the Death Goddess by entering her body. ('The fish of Maui'
    is the North Island of New Zealand, hooked and hauled up
    from the sea bottom by Māui.)
mō for
ngā mōkai captives, pet birds or animals; a term applied to the youngest
    members of a family. Baxter used it to mean 'the fatherless ones'.
Moko facial tattoo

Ngāti-Hiruharama the Jerusalem iwi (literally, this could be only a
    hapū [sub-tribe] of Ngāti Hau, so the expression probably
    refers to the members of Baxter's community)

[315]

o of, belongs to, from

pā a village, originally fortified
pākehā New Zealander of non-Māori descent
pātaka store-house for food
pia beer
pōrangi mad; madman
he pōrangi, he tūtūā a madman, a nobody
pūkeko bird found on wetlands; swamp-hen
punga tree-fern

Te Ra the sun (by extension, God)
Te Ra rite tonu Te Atua The sun who is like the Lord
rīwai potato

taku ngākau ki a koe I give my heart to you
Te Tama boy, son, God the Son (by extension)
Tāne Mahuta a giant kauri tree in Waipoua Forest
Tangaroa god of the sea
tāniko woven cloak, band or belt
taniwha spirit or demon
ka tīmata te pupuhi o te hau the wind began blowing
tuatara reptile resembling a large lizard
tūtūā worthless, a nobody

Wāhi Ngaro the Void, Space (a term used in Maori creation chants),
    world of God and spirits
waiata song
He Waiata mō Te Kare Song for Te Kare
te whare kēhua the haunted house
wharepuni meeting-house, principal dwelling
Te Whiro Death
Te Whiti Born in Ngāmotu, Taranaki, in 1830, Te Whiti o Rongomai
    was a religious prophet and leader of Te Atiawa who advocated
    a policy of passive resistance at the time of the confiscation of
    Taranaki lands by the Europeans. The community he established
    at Parihaka was destroyed by British troops in 1881. He died in 1907.

Index of first lines

[317]

[318]

[321]

[323]

[324]

When four years old he fell asleep between   24
When I go among the trees, up the path you know well,   304
When I stayed those three months at Macdonald Crescent   283
When I was only semen in a gland   111
When the mine exploded at Kaitangata   96
When Tim and I stumbled   32
When you hammered the spigot in, Fitz,   165
Where the sighing combs of water   138
While bluegum fables burn   55
Winter unbundles a sack of storms   75

Yes; I know the steep street well   30
Yesterday I planted garlic,   240
You had tied green leaves around your head;   184
You may be sure no matron will ever row out   167
You will see him light a cigarette   20
'You'll have to learn,' said Uncle Sam,   132

Index of titles

[329]

[330]